Born in Bristol in 1960 ... at the age of 15 and worked as a shopgirl. She was taken back home, but at 16 returned to London to work for *New Musical Express*, which was recruiting young untried writers. She has since graduated to *New Society, The Literary Review, Time Out, The Face,* and the *Sunday Times,* and become a much-loved/much-loathed essayist.

LOVE IT OR SHOVE IT

Julie Burchill

CENTURY PUBLISHING

LONDON

Copyright © Julie Burchill 1985

First published in Great Britain in 1985
by Century Publishing Co. Ltd,
Portland House,
12–13 Greek Street, London W1V 5LE

Burchill, Julie
    Love it or shove it.
    1. Great Britain——Social conditions——1945–
    I. Title
    941.085'8   HN385.5

ISBN 0 7126 0746 3

Filmset by Deltatype, Ellesmere Port
Printed and bound in Great Britain
by Guernsey Press Co Ltd, Guernsey, Channel Islands

The author would like to thank Amy Jenkins and Jon Savage for their help, Peter York for his patronage and Cosmo Landesman for everything.

Contents

Acknowledgements

The articles and reviews in this collection first appeared as
follows:

'Last Days of the Locust', *The Face*, November 1983; 'Randy
Mandy and Simon Said', *The Face*, May 1984; 'Working-Class
Neros', *New Musical Express*, 24 November 1979; 'King
Bunny', *The Literary Review*, November 1984; 'Lush Life',
New Society, March 1984; 'Food for Faith', *Sunday Times*,
November 1984; 'Housewives' Choice', *Sunday Times*,
September 1984; 'Aunts in Your Pants', *Sunday Times*, May
1984; 'Idols on Parade', *The Face*, March 1984; 'Revolutions
Per Minute', *Time Out*, October 1984; 'The Rage is Beige',
Time Out, November 1984; 'The Hype Type', *Sunday Times*,
June 1984; 'The Same Old Con', *Time Out*, October 1984;
'Better Cred Than Dead', *The Face*, 1984; 'Old Bores'
Almanac', *New York Rocker* April 1984; 'Soft Cells', *Sunday
Times*, August 1984; 'Genocide', *The Face*, November 1981;
'Falklands: No Island is an Island, *The Face*, June 1982; 'A
Christmas Wish: The End of America', *The Face*, January 1984;
'Greeneland Revisited', *The Face*, August/September 1983; and
'Waiting for the Russian Ballet', *The Danube*, Autumn 1984.

The author would like to thank the various publishers for
permission to reprint them.

Thanks also to Enoch Powell, MP for permission to quote
from his speech at South Down in October 1983, and to Mr
Graham Greene and The Bodley Head for permission to quote
from his novels.

How I Learned to Stop Worrying and Loathe the Proletariat

I was sitting on a sofa somewhere in SW1, St James or so, very
quietly, minding my own business, when a Churchill sat
down next to me, introduced herself — Emma Soames — and
asked me to write something for the literary magazine she had
just taken the wheel of. 'Oh, *pleeeze*, Julie,' she said
enthusiastically. 'You would do it *soo* well!'

PLEASE! She didn't have to say PLEASE! For one moment I
was ready to beg her to ask *more* of me. Make me review an
Angela Carter book! Send me single-handed onto the beaches
of Normandy to face the dread legions of Günter Grass,
Alberto Moravia and Yukio Mishima fans with only a copy of
Pride and Prejudice for cover fire! ANYTHING, EMMA! FOR I AM
A BRITON AND YOU ARE A CHURCHILL AND MY ONLY FUNCTION
IS TO SERVE YOUR GLORIOUS GENES!

So I shrugged and said, 'OK.'

It was an interesting encounter, for me though probably not
for Emma Soames, to whom one conniving hack probably
looks much like another one. Surely English society had come a
long way, baby, if an actual *Churchill* could sit down on a sofa
next to the little counter-jumper daughter of two factory hands,
who had given up school as a bad job at fifteen and flounced
off to sell scent in swinging London, and ask her, ever so nicely
and enthusiastically — pleeeze! — to do her a favour. A cat
may not only look at a king these days, but a brat may look at a
Churchill and say, very casually, 'OK', and receive many
thanks.

On the other hand, I knew that the girls I had gone to school
with would never believe that far away, in London, in literary
society, in SW1, Churchills and erstwhile shopgirls could have

casual conversations. As a teenager, the print still wet behind my ears, I would go back to my hometown and see my friends and they would ask me how I was doing, what I was up to. Not bragging, merely impressed and excited, I would tell them that some MP or other had written to me and asked me to the House; some cousin or other of the Queen had called up and asked me to dinner. And they would look at me half bemused, half contemptuous, as though humouring an idiot, as though I had just claimed to have sprouted wings. And they would say, they would always say, '*Stop* it. Stop messing about. Seriously. What have you been doing?'

I know the working class, the new working class, and I know their fatalism and their tiny minds. I know they believe that things were never any different from the way they are now, and I know they believe they can never be different. I know that in this country you can live and die and never meet a person from outside your social class apart from in a purely commercial context — the fellatrix, the fishmonger, the physician. I know that this is the only country in Europe, or in the English-speaking world, where accent is determined more by class than region — all men are equal until they open their mouths. Only in Britain does accent command more respect than money or education. I know that the cross-class romance is as rare and disapproved of in this country as the cross-race romance; from the Abdication to Marianne Faithfull, it is bound to end in tears. I know I never met a person who was not working class, doctors and teachers apart, till I lived in London at the age of fifteen. I know that peasant mothers in El Salvador often carve the sign of the cross into the clitoris of a baby girl with a razor blade 'so as to make her a better worker and stop her from getting ideas' and while I know this is not normal practice in Britain, I also know that working-class people bring up their children without hope, with horrifically hemmed in horizons, with a savage lack of faith. I know that for years I believed the working class inherently superior to other people, and now I know they're not and it *hurts*, it hurts like hell. The working class were my religion, and I know I have lost my faith.

I believe there was once a wonder drug they said would cure

the crippling class segregation this country has always suffered from; it was called the Sixties, and great claims were made for it. Class mobility, meritocracy, that sort of thing. But the Sixties were the decade that *shattered* the working class, dazzled them and made Darwinians of them. In the Sixties the class war ostensibly stopped, but really the gloves came off and the dirty work went on. In the Sixties the British people became as newborn babes, a people with collective amnesia, and while this might sound sort of fresh and nice it was the undoing of the proletariat. Only knowledge of their past, and the strength they had shown, and the victories they had won, ensured their future; and they gave up this, their political power for their spending power, their role as prole for their role as consumer. The eagerness with which they went back to Tory rule after giving Labour only six years in which to create a new nation, a Jerusalem-on-Thames, was wimpy enough; but electing Eden, Churchill and Macmillan were acts of political sophistication compared to their election — four times — of Harold Wilson. This man Wilson did for the Labour Party what Jack Kennedy did for the American Democratic Party: made it the poor man's Tory/Republican party, cheap charisma standing in for bulldog breeding. Harold Wilson made it seem as though There Was No Alternative; you were a rich Tory or a poor Tory, and if you were a poor Tory you voted Labour. He shook colour TVs before the eyes of the electorate as colonisers shook glass beads before natives, and the coloured glass worked its white man magic once more. The Sixties were a lazy, greedy decade during which the working class completely frittered away the chance the post-War disorder had given them to redefine their requirements from society. The white flag they waved, though, to give them their due, was a dazzlingly clean one, thanks to the new twin-tub washing machine, and it didn't seem to matter much that the only Triumph they would ever have was a motorbike.

The English Sixties, unlike the American Sixties, were not years of idealism but years of cynicism, in which the ideals of a hundred years were traded in for immediate and gimmicky gratification. England grew no new concerns to replace the old ones, either; CND died the death, English girls were too busy being dollybirds to be feminists — American Negroes got the Freedom Riders, English Negroes got Christine Keeler. And the class shake-up people talked about was a con, typical of the conman decade. The working class in the shape of their carefully selected youth — Twiggy, the Beatles (note the gonky, punny names) — were patronised for their cute, comic accents, little trolls to cut out and collect, and told that the world was their oyster. Of course, all that really happened was that the young working class continued to pour into sport and entertainment to escape their grisly fate as they had since the year dot; and it just so happened that the sensation-seeking eye of the American-speaking media was on London in order to immortalise the Christine Keeler Story in the same year as the Beatles' first record and the Shrimp's first photograph. Suddenly it seemed that Britain was composed solely of sexually active, beautiful young beings from below stairs; the international eye lingered on these latest clowns at the court of St James and pronounced it a classless youth revolution. But they were only jesters, only window dressing, wielding as much power as a shoal of showroom dummies.

Bang the bell, Jack, *I'm* on the bus. The Sixties was the decade when bootstrap idealism was born-again British; when one, if the tongue was slippery enough, could make personal greed sound like political theory. The Sixties were survivalist, a throwing off of historical class loyalties; they were when Margaret Thatcher, a woman, a Northerner, a poor girl from a grammar school who before the War would have been perfect firebrand Socialist material, settled into Parliament, sitting comfortably in her Swinging London constituency, ensconced with her family in groovy Chelsea, just off the King's Road. Swinging Darwinian London, Daddy-O. Mrs Thatcher was a monster of the Sixties, like those other low-born high-rising destroyers Hyams, Kagan, Miller; there was no other decade in which she could have recognised her capacity for selfishness and ambition and still be thought decent. With her degree and her divorcee in Chelsea, London, England, Margaret was truly a Sixties girl. Julie Christie in *Darling*; take away the beauty and

4

substitute the beast and the stories are the same. The arriviste had arrived in the only decade it could be its bloodthirsty self in.

Who was Mrs Thatcher's hero? Who was her role model for her startlingly odd and new code of political conduct? She has never admitted it — not even to herself — but I would bet it was Harold Wilson, who became leader of the Opposition during the years that Mrs Thatcher first held minor office. Sometimes, perhaps, she would look across the floor and see him, sucking smugly yet suggestively on his pipe; scientific man, material man — white hot Sixties man. Harold Wilson, even more than Jean Shrimpton — who with her high smooth debutante brow and huge anxious eyes looked more like a Thirties society girl wondering whether she should run off with her boyfriend and be a nurse for the Spanish Republicans than the zany zeitgeist she was supposed to be — *looked* like the Sixties, impossibly gluttonous and self-satisfied, a man without tradition and history to clutter up his head; a man in control, albeit of a vehicle speeding up a cul-de-sac. He never looked worried or sick or tired, not like the post-war Tory aristocrats who often looked as though they wanted nothing more than to sit down and THINK about where their country was going (probably because they knew so much about where it had been, and how brave it had been, and how precious it was; Eden and Macmillan were both Etonians who had been wounded and decorated copiously in the First World War, who had resigned from office over Conservative Government acceptance of Fascist Italy's invasion of Ethiopia between the Wars, and who had come to the end of their political careers in disgrace due to their sense of honour and fair play more fitting to the playing fields of their old school than their new England — going into Suez to protect his country and the new Jews' country from a man he saw, through a Benzedrine panic, as a newer, darker Hitler; believing Mr Profumo's profuse lies). Wilson was perfect for a country that wanted to kid itself that it had no caste and no past; the high-powered Hovis accent (anyone can be Prime Minister), the constant technobabble (perfect for the English distrust of intellectuals — a precursor of the current Tory technology eggs-in-one-basket faith-healing), his promotion of have-nots,

5

his social contract (put away your glorious red and gold in mothballs, Friar T.U.C). Mr Wilson reassured his electorate that he had not got beyond page three of *Das Kapital*. He was a born (again) leader. He was a disgrace. Harold Wilson was the first Labour leader without a dream; his only dream was realised the day he became Labour leader.

Between Wilson and Thatcher the people elected Heath — a would-be throwback, a Penge local council nova imitating the bothered and bewildered post-war blue-blood warrior worriers, pulped by the unions — and tolerated Callaghan, Lennie to Mr Wilson's George, who went the same way. To bring down the government had become the prerogative of the intellectually bankrupt trade union, and it felt good, the collective expression of the brute force of the powerless — smash a phone box, smash a government. It was not ideal behaviour, but it was preferable to consumerist contentment, which seemed the only other option. The Seventies, though, were a decade of stopping the clock, taking stock, and somewhere along the line the cartwheels had to stop. The working class suddenly scared themselves; they drew in their collective breath (the belt would come later). After the first decade in which the working class, in the shape of union muscle, had had the power and the gumption to say yes or no to government policy, and had said no frequently and loudly and long, the working class felt they were teetering on the precipice — on the edge of what they chose to call anarchy, the big bad non-comprendez wolf, but which was really *power*. They were frightened of their own power and the responsibility, the hard work it would bring. Truly, as the bigots say, the British working man was frightened of hard work.

Somewhere in the Seventies, if the working class had wished it, they were strong enough to pull it all off, pull it all down. But their *vice Anglais*, their desire to be bullied and led by their betters, got the better of them. The working class felt that they had become demonic hedonists, all because they had acquired a fondue set; they felt they had had too good a time in the Sixties, because they had been told it was the decade of Spend Spend Spend and Live Now Pay Later. For a few lousy cars

6

and fridges, the Puritan in the English character (the Welsh and the Scots never fell for Thatcher) blamed itself rather than the Government for the country's slowdown, externalising its own supposed laziness and greediness onto its most visible face — the unions.

The Seventies were a decade of nostalgia; for the Gatsby Twenties, for the Mosley Thirties, for the Glenn Miller Forties. The Seventies started with *Upstairs, Downstairs*, nostalgia for order, and ended with punk, nostalgia for ANGER. Because somewhere when they were never having had it so good, the working class had forgotten HOW TO FEEL ANGER. Now all they could feel were remorse and guilt. The Seventies were spent hiding from the future in costume drama and culminated in the election of Mrs Thatcher; the working-class people who voted for her hoped she would send Us back below stairs and teach Us a lesson, thus saving the beloved country. She put the responsibility for British decline firmly on the shoulders of the British, as opposed to the shoulders of the Americans and the Arabs whose fault it really was — the one militarily and morally, the other financially. And the British loved it. She blamed the British worker, and the British worker voted for her. She blamed the trade unionists, and they voted for her, too. *Le vice Anglais* came to the fore in British party politics for the first time, and we voted with our groins. And to lead us, we had at last neither the doddering lord of the manor nor the demobbed Father Christmas, but the dominatrix in the pussy-cat bow, the Darwinian Dresden doll.

In the Sixties, no one talked about class, except to say it didn't exist any more. The working class, in the guise of their young, had the dynamism that made Britain if not great then F.A.B. But now the young as a whole are seen as stateless, rootless, displaced persons, and everyone knows which class they are, with deadly accuracy. Who could have foreseen in the Sixties that class, and the defining of it, would one day be a major industry? That one day being YOUNG or being OLD would stop sufficing as to whether you were IN or OUT? Now Britain is comprised of YAPS, Young Fogeys, Noovs, Nouveaux Pauvres and Sloane Rangers, and William Hamilton, no less, will not stand for Parliament again but will write a book about the class system in this country, with the Royal Family making a cameo appearance as The Root Of All Evil.

Come the hour, come the tout, *tout suite*. But the new class awareness is not just a cute idea fit to shift some units; it is a particularly dirty fact of life. After six years of Mrs Thatcher's rule, her electorate are chronically shifted, sorted and pigeon-holed; signed on, sealed up and delivered into the land of plenty of nothing — just what they always wanted. The symptoms of the new class sickness are everywhere: from the savagely revived North-South divide to the Royal revival; from the new terrible use of heroin, that marathon suicide note, by the working-class young to bingo in the newspapers of the powerless; from docility in the face of unemployment to the lack of English working-class support for the miners. This is still the only country in the English-speaking world or Europe where accent is determined by class rather than region — people still gauge POWER by accent rather than by wealth or educational credentials. Education still counts for nothing in this country, if you don't talk as your betters talk; and if you DO talk this way, you can be as dim as you wish and still rise (or at least tread water). The power and poignancy of the Diana Spencer Story comes from the fact that she was a teenage school-leaver from a one-parent family with not one CSE to her name — like a million English girls on the scrap-heap, young ladies in waiting for a job that will never show — yet landed the cushiest, best-paid apprenticeship in the country because of the way she talked. Sensing this exclusive force field, the lowest proportion of working-class students in the white Western world enter universities in Britain, though it is the only system that works on a grant rather than loan basis — surely conducive to the comfort of lower earners? But no; they know there is no point.

No point; no encouragement either. Perhaps the worst thing about the working class in this country is the lack of encouragement they give their children to try something new, something non-manual. They are cruel in their lack of constructive advice, but to give them the benefit of the doubt, perhaps they are simply fearful that if their glottal-stopping

8

offspring fly too high they will crash too hard on the rocks of rejection. On the other hand, it could be because of their lack of respect for themselves and their own kind, their own blood; a lack of respect which goes hand in hand with the grovelling adoration currently given to the House of Windsor — those modern gods for a soulless, secular society, those 'icons of cleanliness', as Anthony Burgess brilliantly called them, for a society which feels guilty and dirty.

The awful mawkish excitement over the Royal babies: the beggars on the streets, asking for money to buy 'Food for the baby' — it could be the Twenties, or another country. It is not a *civilised* country any more, for sure. It is ungracious to harp on about the Windsors, poor Hun, because they did not choose to be born useless, and some of them seem quite nice — but it is partly their fault that Britain is as it is, that it is not dynamic or powerful. It is not *healthy* for a country to have such a LUMP in it, such a large tribe at the TOP, who are not particularly intelligent or attractive and yet cannot slip down the social scale to the position their mediocrity best suits them for simply because of where they were BORN. They are a blockage in the national system, and they make ridiculous any idea of a meritocracy — that people succeed if they work hard and fail if they don't — thus discouraging initiative in many people, and driving many more abroad to English-speaking countries where region and not class determines accent. It is less King Arthur who is responsible for the laziness of the British worker than Queen Elizabeth.

Perhaps the most pathetic part of the English working-class attitude towards the Family is the belief that if they were to retire gracefully to a State pension and a row of bijou cottages in Fulham, then England would automatically lose the little revenue it makes from the tourist trade. What a disgraceful lack of faith in one's country, and what atrocious disrespect to London, the most beautiful city in the non-Communist world! The innate belief that worshipping the Windsors somehow makes us more 'civilised' than non-believers is incredibly ill-sorted, and it stands up very badly once you look beyond the doll's house that Britain has become to the rest of the world;

9

according pomp, ceremony and servility to your Royal family is not a trait found anywhere else in the world apart from the horribly underdeveloped countries of Africa, where appalling waddling monarchs, whose fat the people could live off for a year, bustle to and fro being regal. Of course there are other monarchies in the world; but they are the bicycle monarchies of cool, rich Scandinavia and the Low Countries, where the King may hail his own taxi at the airport, or the Ambre Solaire monarchy of Monaco, where the beautiful princess pushes her own luggage through the terminal. The only arrogant, worshipped monarchies in the world exist in Britain and Africa: and they are synonymous not with civilisation but with superstition, stupidity and educational subnormality. There is never any excuse to worship, unless you are a Zulu who doesn't know any better.

The pathetic popularity of the Windsors is matched only at the moment by the unpopularity of the miners. The miners' strike of 1984, which looks as though it will last for a year at least, was a watershed in the measurement and comprehension of working-class cowardice. In 1926 the miners' strike led to the General Strike of May 4th to May 12th, which, while diminutive, at least *dared*; the striking miners of 1984 were supported by a bewildering array of fans — from John Paul Getty Junior, who donated copious thousands to their families, to such shimmering starlets as Sade and Wham and half the world's entertainers who play benefits for them ceaselessly, from the Haldane Society of Lawyers to Sinn Fein, from Colonel Qaddafi to St Mary's Hospital Social Club of West London, from the PLO to Goldsmith's College; a boy I know at Brasenose College said you could always spot an Oxford Etonian — he'd be the one collecting for the Miners' Fund — but not by one fellow union, in the only way a union can *really* exercise power: by going on strike. Even the French unions, the *French*, sent everything but the *cuisine couler* to the pit communities for the Christmas of 1984. It sometimes seemed that everyone in the world supported the miners — except for the Tories and the British working-class.

The bravery and defiance of the striking miners were

admirable; their aims, though, were not, and further served to illustrate the paradoxical wilderness the post-war working-class had wandered into. To see the Government win would be awful — but if and when the miners win, what do they want? And is what they want *good for them*? For years miners wanted nothing more than for their children *not* to follow them, to have education, to move up into the light. Suddenly it seems that all they want is a guarantee that their children and grandchildren will lead the same dark, blind life they led.

In supporting the miners, the good, the glitterati and the gullible showed their nostalgia for a life that never was, and never could be; another example of class amnesia, every pit village a Hovis heaven of happy families and true hearts. But the mining communities so romanticised by the Left are, when in working order, bastions of everything the Left intensely and presently loathes. Whiteness; strictly differentiated male and female roles (it is funny to see London's feminist women involving themselves in Miners' *Wives Support* Groups, where in any other circumstance, a woman being described as someone's *wife* or *support* would be proscribed as Fascism); wage slavery; the equation of any sort of male sensitivity with homosexuality. The calls of certain sweet Labour aristocrats for the mining community and the homosexual community to 'support each other's struggle', not to mention the PITS AND PERVERTS FUND-RAISING NIGHTS, starring the brilliant Bronski Beat and staged by 'Lesbians And Gays Support The Miners', had a real pathos; as though a single gay or lesbian from the mining community could *ever* have come out and *been themselves*, and continued to live in a pit village.

From the point of view of the genuinely underprivileged sections of society, who realised that they were still being treated like sick imbeciles after the war that everyone believed would make everyone happy, the break up of English working-class community is, sadly, a wonderful thing. Females, coloureds, inverts — there is no room in the annals of working-class prejudice for the pride of these. Even in the corridors of power, this sad truth echoes; Labour is the whitest, malest, most heterosexual party in Parliament, while the chairman of the All-

Party Gay Group is a Tory, the only coloured MP is a Tory, the first female MP was a Tory and, as we know to our cost, the first female PM was a Tory.

I wish I was a coloured female invert and could speak for the undernation as a whole, but I can only speak as a female; and in my view, it has been proved conclusively that the rights of women do not go hand in glove with the dawn of socialism. The working-class 'extended family' of feminist socialist legend *really* meant a working-class girl with no home of her own, living in fear of her mother-in-law; the break up of the old pre-war working-class communities freed women from fear of what the neighbours would say to a great extent. After the Cuban revolution, in which women played a great part, Fidel Castro exhorted them to go back to breeding and feeding; yet Eva Peron ruled Argentina. The *striving* mood of women is more in tune with the striving ideas of the Right — no Communist country has been led by a woman so far, whereas Right-wing democracies and dictatorships have — than with the Left, whose women are still held back in *support*; stifling, dulling, deadly support. Despite what Ken Livingstone may wake up screaming/dreaming, the interests of the weak, reluctantly oppressed — females, coloureds, inverts — and the muscly, voluntarily oppressed — the working-class — are almost entirely opposed. It is chilling; it hurts; but it has to be said — the English working-class getting of wisdom: IT NEVER REALLY HAPPENED. Our precious past is an optical, optimistic illusion.

In 1981, well into Thatched Britain, a survey showed that 86 per cent of Britons trusted the police, 81 per cent trusted the army, 76 trusted God, while 72 *dis*trusted the trade unions. IS THAT ALL THERE IS? Yes: my mother holding out her hands to the TV screen for what she supposed was warmth one cold night, the two to one working-class electorate who voted in Mrs Thatcher not once but twice, twice, for eight whole years. One cold night leads to eight whole years of the Stupidity Crusade; Mrs Thatcher, the game-show PM. Double or quits; the faith healer.

Have the working class changed since they emerged from the glorious Second World War, heroic and raring to go? They are richer and they are less intelligent. They learn more and know less. They are still as *powerless*, which is really what divides the men from the drones, and the classes from each other. They are more cowardly than they were, and when times are hard, they will not organise against the people who made times hard — their rulers — but pick on each other, dividing and sub-dividing like suicidal amoebas, passing the bad-luck buck. They are incredibly politically ignorant and prejudiced; nowhere else in Europe is the word 'Communist' on a par with 'cannibal' or 'child-fucker'.

I see no end to this state of affairs, and no big shift back to Labour. In a way, the working class have come home; the Tories are the natural party of the under-educated, and their brash, anti-idealistic, anti-cerebral world-view appeals to the suspicious, fatalistic working man — voting Tory is as easy and mindless as supporting a football team. Myself, after years of resistance (calling lunch dinner; calling dinner tea), I too am turning my back on my heritage and my roots in true modern style and receiving instruction in the discreet charm of the bourgeoisie. Bang the bell, Jack (as the Cockneys say) — I'm on the bus. Or at least on a sofa somewhere in SW1.

Last Days of the Locust

I walk along the street of sorrows/The Boulevard of Broken Dreams/Where Gigolo — and Gigolette/Can take a kiss — without regret/So they forget their broken dreams/You laugh tonight and cry tomorrow/When you behold your shattered schemes/And Gigolo — and Gigolette/Wake up and find their eyes are wet/With tears that tell of broken dreams . . .
Here is where you'll always find me/Always walking up and down/But I left my soul behind me/In an old Cathedral town/The joy that you find here you borrow/You cannot keep it long it seems/But Gigolo — and Gigolette/Still sing a song/And dream along/The Boulevard of Broken Dreams.
Song from the 1934 Warners musical *Moulin Rouge*, excised by order of Jack Warner — 'Too depressing!'

Whenever a new Bananarama single sashays into the marketplace, a peculiar kind of drool emits from certain pilots of the airwaves; drooling that is a world away from the histrionic admiration aped for, say, Kim Wilde and, once, Debbie Harry. Newsmen and technicians are asked over to the microphone and the DJ will ask them which one they 'want'. '*Give me that one!*' 'I like that one!' '*Who's that one — Keren!*'

There is a singular kind of disrespect accorded to Bananarama within the music business: they are PRETTY GIRL SINGERS who do not PLAY INSTRUMENTS (being able to *play an instrument* is of crucial importance to the Boys Brigade, Muse-Biz Branch) or write all of their own songs (the Belle Stars, spectacularly untalented, have been able to evade the leering and sneering Bananarama are subjected to because they fill both these qualifications, albeit poorly). And PRETTY GIRL

SINGERS are meant to have Svengalis and protectors — Miss
Wilde's father and brother very much in evidence, Miss Harry's
boyfriend forever lurking behind her — they are meant to have
a *brand*, a Keep Off, a Property Of. And if she does not bear a
brand, even today, an attractive young female singer will be fair
game for the creepiest of verbal kerbcrawling.

It is well-documented that Bananarama first came to fame
because the Fun Boy Three saw a picture of them, liked them
— who wouldn't? — and wanted to make a record with them.
To the old boys of the business — who despite the trappings,
the pruning of hair and flares, are all still very much pay-your-
dues trad dads — this kind of entry to the Big Time must have
seemed amazingly Hollywood. '*Hey, baby, you wanna be in
pictures?*' It must have been this innocent beginning which led
Bananarama to the unenviable niche they occupy today.

This is obviously a fabricated case — Bananarama's appeal
and selling points are obvious, they have a fresh paint beauty
and an awkwardness that appeals to beautifully painted but
awkward teenage girls, who I would imagine make up the
majority of their public. But it got me thinking about the ancient
tradition of the Svengali-Trilby set-up, and how rock and roll
inherited it wholesale from Hollywood, and I found it fascinating
— not the above-board black fairytales about Spector and
Ronnie and Gordy and Ross, but the darker stories, the more
illicit, desperate Sugar Daddies. Because, of course, rock and
roll has always been a boy's business, and the sheer glut of boys
involved means that many Trilbies have been non-girls.

This area of activity has been documented little, probably
because it spoils the picture of male demand and female supply,
probably because the homoerotic impulse of rock is as
embarrassing to acknowledge as that of football – it's just too
close to home. The moguls of Hollywood were the biggest
bunch of heterosexual Philistines ever to hire a secretary
because of the speed at which she could undress rather than
take dictation, and this development would have bothered
them, but in every other way they would have recognised the
rock and roll rumble from its start to the point where the power
passed from the Svengalis to the precocious singer-songwriter as

15

their own torrid turf.

Somewhere in the Fifties, when the film industry was in its forties, middle-aged, Hollywood stopped being H*O*L*L*Y*W*O*O*D and became a place of business, worried, respectable, somewhat ulcerous like any other businessman fallen on hard times. There was TV. There were the agents — Kurt Frings, who represented Audrey Hepburn and Elizabeth Taylor, amongst others, was often called The Man Who Killed Hollywood — who helped actors escape from long-term studio contracts and negotiated them huge fees for one film at a time — Frings got Taylor her cool, notorious million for *Cleopatra* — that eventually killed the studio machine and the spirit of Hollywood.

Actors, schooled in the Method East, became awkward and autonomous, unwilling to use their bodies as hard currency. The swarthy boys off the boat, who brought Hollywood to bloom upon the California desert as other, braver Jews would do in Palestine, were dead and their beloved companies passed into the hands of genteel Gentile corporations with none of the steel and sentimentality it takes to make a great film.

The greatest goldrush town of all time, the heart that called the lonely hunters from all over the world was all gone bar the Hollywood Sign. *Something* had to come along that was as epic, as shoddy, as greedy, as naive, as cruel, as corrupt, as desperate as the dead magnet. Some splendid, sordid shanty town that would unite under the banner of AMBITION the very tender, the very tough, the very talented, the very tarnished.

In the Fifties Locustland moved location, and Sammy Glick changed horses. And they called it rock and roll.

The new boomtown started not with a sneer — nor even a kiss curl — but a whimper: Johnny Ray, half-deaf, depressed, religious, sensitive, shallow, alcoholic, ridiculous and more hysterically loved than any man since Valentino. It was Ray who turned the tide of popular music: from the Voice to the Act — pop's roots are not in popular music but in the performances of charismatic freaks: not Glenn Miller and Bing Crosby but James Dean and Aimee Semple McPherson — from the Singer

16

— Sinatra, Bennett — to the Showman, from eliciting restrained admiration from one's fans to provoking them to ever more hysterical attacks by one's own hysterical behaviour — Ray was knocked unconscious twice by those who loved him most; very West, very Locust.

He burst into tears as he sang 'Cry' or 'The Little White Cloud That Cried' and he banged his head against the piano when it all got too much for him. He was the Jayne Mansfield of pop, totally numb and unautonomous and out of control with no redeeming merit whatsoever — no voice, no songs, no music. But by 1953 he was earning more than $150,000 a week, around twice what a popular studio-contracted film star could earn for a film taking around three months to make.

His self-confessed freakishness coupled with his tremendous success made sure that the tone of POP was set forever as terminally hysterical; boomtown hysterical, goldrush hysterical. It was seen that by getting up in front of seemingly normal people and thrusting your wounds in their faces, they might make you a millionaire in a moment.

This was something new in music, and this was pop; Johnny Ray catered more to the need that had sent the paying public on guided gaping tours around Bedlams than the need which had set a million feet moving to Glenn Miller. Glenn Miller catered to a healthy physical desire, Bedlam to a sick appetite, and pop with its never-ending parade of freaks leant more towards Bedlam. It was no accident that Colonel Tom Parker was a former fairground barker. He knew a freak that the public would pay for when he saw one.

'The man who ended it all and started it all,' Virginia Ironside called Ray in an uncommonly inspired moment, and this is the most accurate description yet; before Johnny Ray, mere talent, mere voice was enough, but after Ray you had to be less a singer than an emotion-shower — to be really big you had to be a new kind of freak, a bigger freak than the freak before.

Johnny Ray, the misery freak, was deposed by something even more outrageous than a man who cried — a white male entertainer who moved as though he was used to having sex at a time when every white male entertainer in America acted as

17

though they were anti-matter between the neck and the knees — a sex freak. Ray faded away, the only proof that he had ever existed was the occasional misery freak — Roy Orbison, Gene Pitney — who cropped up in the early Sixties and let the public pay for the privilege of counting their tears.

The sex freaks went in two by two . . . Americans have short memories and Harlow, West, Valentino kept no one awake at night any more: to America Presley and Monroe must have seemed like the first sex freaks in the world. Even when the inane babble about the Body and the Pelvis had died down, no one really got beyond the physical being to the alleged talent; no one ever liked Presley's voice yet found him ugly, no one ever admired Monroe's acting yet found her unattractive.

You fell in love with the shell and pretended you liked the raw, sad, squirming thing inside. No one really reacted to Monroe and Presley as actor and singer but as updated, XXX-rated Gypsy Rose Lees — mass media burlesque deities. So big, so blowsy, so . . . *American*. Surely Britain would never fall?

But post-war Britain, definitively defiled by America, laid back and tried to enjoy it. By the late Fifties, a torrid, tarty, touching time, fair play and knowing one's place were gone for good and SEX, MONEY, VIOLENCE, the *Liberté, Egalité, Fraternité* of Americanism, were here to stay.

Diana Dors wore her mink bikini. Politicians paid to taste the whip. Rachman took his Alsatians for a walk. The country girl Christine Keeler left the tiny village of Wraysbury and took a train to certain fame. The Kray twins were in seventh heaven east eleven. This was the time of the gangster, the spiv and the starlet. These were the opening steps of the dance of culture-death and nothing could have been more normal than the freak parade.

At first it wasn't that way. Jazz could only be bought in the West Indian clubs of West London, like marijuana. The radio played swing slush incessantly, the sort of music that had been popular since the Forties — cheap copies of American bigbands — Ted Heath, Joe Loss, Ronnie Scott — all with obligatory prim, greasy singer out front showing off — Lita Roza, Dennis

18

Lotis, Ronnie Hilton. The music business revolved around the massed publishers' offices of Denmark Street, sheet music still being more important than records; the publishers were married, Jewish, middle-aged, usually blown into popular music from dying Variety — Toytown Harry Cohns, with all the ambition and none of the talent. And they ruled a toytown kingdom called Tin Pan Alley.

The Brill Building, the most famous songwriting factory in America, has been made a legend, a Valhalla of Bronx gods, by distance of time and space; a hive of throbbing teenage Jews hustling luscious youngblood epics, positive walking jukeboxes. The Brill Building had a nasty habit of turning out turkeys by the truckload, but the myth stuck. Tin Pan Alley has never been showered with anything but scorn — but Lionel Bart worked there — 'Living Doll' — and so did John Barry; managers, promoters, publicists ran around Soho from dawn till dusk hustling and grabbing and gab gab gabbing, and Sammy Glick would have felt perfectly at home there.

If you have a hot spot for showbiz capitalism at full self-seeking, shabby-glory throttle then those sordid teeming West One nights, full of hungry young lyricists sitting over stone cold sober cups of coffee at Julie's, waiting for a miracle to materialise on the blank paper before them, cannot help but make you feel that the first singer-songwriter should have been shot on sight, and that Tin Pan Alley was, after its lurid fashion, a thing of beauty.

Nik Cohn, ill-fated illuminati: 'Rock brought in operators who were younger, faster, tougher, cleverer. Most of them were homosexual. They'd see some pretty young boy sitting in a pub and fancy him and sign him up. They'd bed him and then they'd probably very quickly get bored with him. The boy would fade and disappear again. Or every now and then, he would turn out to be a stayer after all, and he'd somehow keep himself afloat.'

Britain never produced a Johnny Ray — a man who cried for a living, from the land of the stiff upper lip? — but the sex freaks were irresistible. J. Arthur Rank set up a factory to turn out Monroes and a variety of gentlemen went into the Elvis industry.

The most successful manufacturer was Larry Parnes, who

19

was not Svengali to a single singing starlet, but had a *stable*, just like the old days — Darryl Zanuck lives and lies! His Elvettes were not so much sex bombs as sex grenades — pout and sigh rather than cut and thrust — but they sold. Parnes treated his boys like the dumbest bimboes that ever lived, giving them ludicrous names the like of which had not been heard since the days of Louise Lovely — Wilde, Keene, Fury, Goode, Power, Eager, Fortune, Justice, Fame, Gentle, Pride; and let us never forget Cuddley Duddley. He made no attempt to find suitable material for his constellation of freaks, just slapped the latest American hit in front of them and left them to cover it to the best of their abilities. They were devoured by the Batley vultures when their pouts began to sag. In short, they were treated like young female entertainers always had been.

It was POP that finally forced the boys down onto the casting couch, made young male entertainers the anonymous, marketable pieces of meat that young female entertainers had always been. They needed no voices, no songs — technology and American cast-offs saw to that; all they needed was a FACE, the long lashes, the pulpy pink lower lip. And hundreds had those faces. It was a buyers' market, and the boys were duly bought.

It was not surprising that homosexuals were attracted to pop post-Elvis. The image of Elvis, rough and young and beautiful, was not traditional heterosexual fantasy — that was something altogether more mysterious and genteel, from Valentino to Sinatra — but it was an age-old homosexual dream. The opportunity not just to be amongst these boys where they gathered to attract attention but to actually make *money* from them as well as make them must have been irresistible. '*Hey baby, you want to be in pictures?*' now had an inverted equivalent — '*Hey, son, you want to be a pop star?*'

There is an early fan club picture of Cliff Richard, supposedly reading a piece of fan mail; his open shirt reveals one rosy pouting nipple which Cliff is, supposedly unselfconsciously, playing with. The image, coy but raw, is pure homosexual skinrag, and the fact that such an obvious piece of gay soft porn found its way onto numerous virginal bedroom walls is a heartbreakingly innocent paradox.

Many of the boys who flocked to Tin Pan Alley and the men who bossed it were ex-merchant seamen, boys who were looking for something, wanderers. Seamen have always had a more flexible attitude to sex than most: there is the old saying, 'On land it's wine, women and song — at sea it's rum, bum and concertina'. The boys were used, but they were users too — there was the chance of at least a hit record, at most a Svengali who would devote everything in himself to you and make you bigger than you could dream.

It is ironic that the act which put the pretty boy singer, the Svengali system and Tin Pan Alley itself out of business was noticed in the standard sweaty, desire-sick casting couch manner.

In October 1961 Brian Epstein was a dapper, 27-year-old homosexual working in his family's electrical retail business — NEMS, in Whitechapel, Liverpool, a shop with a large record department which boasted 'The Finest Selection In The North'. Helping with the weekend rush, three young people came in and asked for a single, 'My Bonnie', by The Beatles, 'with an A'. Epstein had never heard of the Beatles. He made a memo to himself: 'THE BEATLES — CHECK ON MONDAY.'

In the Cavern he saw four boys swathed in leathers and soaked in sweat, fooling around in the darkness at noon. His fantasies realised, Epstein was poleaxed with love. He spoke with Paul and George ('What brings Mr Epstein here?') between sets, but while they were on stage he could not tear his eyes away from John Lennon. He followed them around but when any of them looked him in the eye he blushed. They were flattered by his attention.

But The Beatles were a closed shop, adept at shutting out the rest of the world, and his embarrassment prevented him from asking outright if he could manage them. Finally, at an after-hours meeting at the NEMS shop, Epstein finally spat it out. The Beatles needed a manager, he wanted to do the job. Did they want him?

Silence, then Lennon said, 'Yes'.

Ironically, although it was their rough trade toughness which had attracted his attention, Epstein had to clean them up to make them acceptable — he had to destroy the fantasy to keep the reality intact, close to him. He loved them, devoting endless time to them for little reward. After the first booking he arranged for them at a café on the Dee Estuary, NEMS profit was just over £1.

Talking to The Beatles still terrified him — Lennon made a habit of staring at him, and the more Lennon stared the more Epstein blushed and stammered. Miraculously he found the nerve to ask Lennon to go to Copenhagen with him for the weekend. A friend advised him to go. 'Shut up,' said Lennon, 'Can't you see he's after me?'

But it was soon spring of 1963. John Lennon had a record at Number One and a son still in the maternity ward. Colossal casserole of neuroses that Lennon was, he now felt man enough to be Epstein's boy. Epstein asked again and, although Cynthia Powell Lennon was dumbstruck and Epstein's friends warned him not to jeopardise his position, neither of them could help themselves. They left for Spain where, as Radclyffe Hall would have it, they were not divided.

Being a Beatle was soon an eight days a week job, and they made no time for wives, managers or anyone. Epstein's attentions turned to a young person from Bootle, Billy Ashton, who he bought from his ageing manager, Jed Knibbs, for the princely sum of £50. Epstein made him over and showed him to George Martin, who was less than impressed by the presence of Billy J. Kramer. But Epstein was adamant that 'My Billy' would succeed; he gave him a Lennon-McCartney song, 'Do You Want To Know A Secret', and let George Martin do his stuff, double-tracking and filling in the cracks in Kramer's voice. It got to Number Two.

His Number One, Lennon, was behaving by now towards Epstein with all the moral incontinence of a wife batterer, taking out on his manager all his own poisons and fears. Epstein suffered agonies over his sexuality, kidding himself that his boys knew nothing of it, desperately contriving to keep his treacherous blackmailing tricks out of their way; yet Lennon could say, loudly and coldly in a crowded dressing room when Epstein was fussing, 'Now what shall I call this book of mine? QUEER JEW.' And again Epstein could be in a drying out clinic, as he was many times, and Lennon would send him bouquets bearing such messages as 'You know I love you — I really mean that', inevitably dissolving Epstein into floods of tears.

Came the day when The Beatles, in their pathetic search for the elusive CLASS, preferred the company of well-connected freeloading hippie scumbags to the decent, neurotic, gifted period piece Epstein. A man of soaring emotion but limited vision, he wanted to be the new Larry Parnes and The Beatles, unimpeachably modish, knew this and despised him for it. With Beatlemania about to break, on the brink of the biggest phenomenon that showbusiness had ever seen, he still saw The Beatles as part of a stable of stars — front runners certainly, but members of a stable nevertheless.

A NEMS handout of the time shows all his boys as mere disembodied FACES — The Beatles, Gerry and his Pacemakers, Billy and his Dakotas — all floating around the smiling head of Mr Brian Epstein wearing a schoolmaster's mortar board. Inadvertently Brian Epstein had killed what he loved most, had made passé the Locustland of Tin Pan Alley where, on a good day, there were two score boys for every Svengali.

The Beatles were with the king of the hippie scumbags, the Maharishi Mahesh Yogi, when Epstein was calling the male escort agencies and finding every boy booked due to the late hour (and anyway they would have been sad substitutes for the boys whose company he really wanted) and taking the Carbitrol that brought his sad, successful life to a close.

The starlet/Svengali seesaw side of pop was decimated by The Beatles' impact; young men realised that you did not need thirty years' experience in Light Music to write pop songs and began to write their own, robbing the lyricists, composers and publishers of much of their power, not to mention their pulling power. And young men who *write* as well as *sing* tend to have very high opinions of themselves — I would go as far as to say that there is not one singer-songwriter on two legs who does not think he is a pigging genius — and are therefore less willing to literally prostitute their art; it is very hard to imagine, say, James Taylor being chased around a desk by a walking cigar in a stained suit promising to make him a star, baby.

But the world is full of pretty boys, as Jackie C might say, and also full of lonely gentlemen, and it was inevitable that a few would fall through the safety net the Beatles had spun.

Kenneth Pitt had been associated with La Judy during the dreadful last days in Chelsea, and had gone on to 'discover' Marty Kristian, who he brought from Australia to London and who later found flimsy fame as the prettiest, most simian New Seeker, and Crispian 'I'll Be Bigger Than Elvis' St Peters. He had an eye for pretty boys with tiny talents, but aside from this he could not have been more different from the furtive fumbling Philistines who had prowled Tin Pan Alley.

He met David Bowie in 1965, when Bowie was 19. 'I was looking for someone who could come out of the pop world and be a star as opposed to a guitar cowboy. There were no up-and-coming Tommy Steeles at that time. No one else was learning to juggle, dance and act as well as sing and play guitar. When I saw David for the first time down at the Marquee, I thought he was someone who could be groomed in just the way I had in mind.'

Bowie was not the tough, smart cookie he is today. His press release ambitions at the time were 'to act in a musical and dance in a film' (what, no travelling and meeting people?). He was a self-obsessed, unsuccessful youngster — and the attentions of an artistic gentleman with infinite connections must have seemed heavenly. So he went along with the plans, putative juggling and all.

Bowie lived for two years in the spare bedroom of Mr Pitt's Marylebone flat; it was an achingly respectable and chivalrous relationship. Mr Pitt was taken home to the Home Counties to meet the parents and subsequently became very close to Mr Jones the elder, who he would spend hours discussing David's career with. Mr Jones once wrote to Mr Pitt: 'When he is in town we are happy to know that he is under your watchful and friendly eye.'

24

The young David Bowie was cursed with chronically bad timing, trying on faces so obviously second-hand that no one was interested. He was a beat too late, he was Newley too late, he was Dylan too late: Pitt found him little modelling and dancing jobs from 1966 to 1968. His brief affairs with Buddhism and ballet dancers always led him back to the spare bedroom.

Throughout their four-year association Pitt spent thousands on Bowie's various harebrained schemes, projects that would obviously show no returns whatsoever. But by 1969, when Bowie was still a resounding reject, he was nevertheless mixing with hippies and egomaniacs who told him that all managers were vampires, teeth bloody with teenage talent, and he believed it because he had to blame his failure on someone other than himself. He left Pitt for good, for better or worse, for domestic bliss and world domination and the hangover that follows both.

David 'Bowie' is essentially a shabby person, and no one could have treated Mr Pitt shabbier. Bowie sent him two tickets to Earls Court, rather insulting when you think he was asking a middle-aged man of some refinement to take his chances among 18,000 rabid freaks. All the proof that remains is the photograph on the mantelpiece, signed 'I love you, David'. Old Svengalis never die, they just gaze at their faded photos.

Little shadow of the beat boomtown casting couch remains; in 1977 Tom Robinson told me in great shock of the biggish wheel who boasted in true Denmark Street style, 'You've got to be either Jewish or homosexual to make it as a manager in this business, and I'm both' before attempting to put the make on the youngest and prettiest person in the band.

But this leering dinosaur was hopelessly out of date. McLaren and Rotten, Rhodes and Strummer — those men didn't want to HAVE those boys, they wanted to BE them.

Only two of today's pop starlets — one girl, one not — have used the chaise of shame in pursuit of fame; all in all, pop has never been cosier. People's careers are guided by their fathers (Weller, Wilde), their brothers (Altered Images) and their childhood friends (Spandau Dagger). The essential epic seediness is gone from pop — your average insurance office contains more stories of naked lust, greed and glory.

This is all very nice for the mothers of crooners . . . but when you see the craven comboes scuffling to play for appreciative, toe-tapping Royalty or hear the latest ferret-faced pin-up primping proudly 'No drugs or alcohol! No drugs or alcohol!', don't you feel like bringing up your breakfast? Don't you think that pop has become too much like a cross between a playpen and a gymnasium? Don't you wish that the sweat smelt different, the sour smell of fast living and last stands rather than the healthy whiff of the decaffeinated workout?

Don't you wish for the days of hysteria and hypocrisy — Billy Fury lying down with his microphone onstage and being banned by the city fathers: Adam Faith, nearly strangled when two worshippers caught opposite ends of his silk scarf and tried to pull it off: Terry Dene, unfit for National Service due to mental imbalance, drunk and disorderly and saved by the Salvation Army.

Those were the days . . . the old freakshow days when pop stars were well-paid pariahs, medicine shows, cheap potent patent medicine, the old days of Salvation and suicide. Pop has been taken to the cleaners, see, and the soiled sideshow soul of it has been scoured away without trace. You would think it was never dirty in its life. But you can't launder a memory, and how many memories must play in the heads of once-powerful sedentary spivs and middle-aged boys with long eyelashes and dashed dreams, about those days behind closed doors in dear dead Tin Pan Alley, those days when the last days of Sodom came to Soho.

Randy Mandy and Simon Said

In recent weeks two (true) gentlemen have made me presents of a brace of choice items of tack, both of which pleased me to an extent that other girls are only moved unto when *that little something* arrives in the hands of a man from Securicor. One was *The Simon Dee Book* and the other was *The Mandy Report*: forget *The Necrophiliacs*, forget *Goodbye Baby And Amen* — these are the two absolutely definitive documents of the Sixties and of the callous, kinky, charming children spawned by them.

We are all steeped in the Profumo Affair by now; it is as luridly British a tale as the abdication or the Koo Stark Story. Britain is *the* country of sex-power scandals — from Parnell to Parkinson — because British people are brought up believing that passion is not their forte, not built into the national character (whatever *that* is), and when desire hits them it really makes them go ape. They just are not prepared for it, they risk everything and invariably they lose everything. The Profumo Scandal is such a British institution, such a perfect British event — sex + class + spies + Communism + sadism: *that's* the stuff the British are really keen on, forget all that crafty disinformation that says we talk about the weather and drink tea. There really should have been a board game based on it in existence for the last 20 years, something as starchy and acceptable as Monopoly. 'Peter Rachman takes his Alsatians for a walk: pay all you own or go directly to hospital.' 'Christine Keeler asks you if her seams are straight: pass Go and collect £200.'

See Mandy. See Mandy talk. See Mandy sell. See Mandy tell. If she had not known Christine the K it is doubtful that Mandy Rice-Davies would have made much of herself — been made much, yes, but not made much of — but as it was she had the luck of the devil/the decade. It was Christine who did the dirty work, Christine who was pilloried. Yet she ended up in World's End penury while Mandy became a real little cottage industry, capable of turning her plump little pink little hand to anything.

'I am not proud of this report. It is, in fact, a wicked, wicked story. It is the sorry tale of a young girl, barely more than a child, baited with mink and diamonds until trapped in a web of complete moral depravity. It is the truth, at long last, about the snakepit masquerading under the title High Society.'

This is the opening of *The Mandy Report* and already Mandy is lying through her badly-capped teeth. 'Baited'! — 'Trapped'! At least one millionaire of her early acquaintance spent many evenings with her offering her the bus fare back to Brum and the quiet life he felt she was designed for. Mandy was a carnivore, never a victim; whereas Christine Keeler simply stood there and let her incredible beauty lead her into all sorts of beds and bedlams — a 'sex zombie', some social commentator once called her — Mandy had to *pursue*, that most unfeminine of activities, that most unforgivable of sins. No wonder she felt the need to pretend. *The Mandy Report* is a sumptuous feast of deception, self and otherwise.

Delight in: Mandy's appallingly *refeened* writing style ('I have been branded a cheap prostitute. That is not so. I am an expensive courtesan if you like, but never a prostitute' — gosh, sorry, Your Majesty); the hard Marxist analysis ('I freely admit that I came to London at the age of 15 eager to catch the sparkle of diamonds on my working-class hands'); the pathos (Mandy's custom-built chassis washed up on some anonymous candlewick motel bedspread); the stirring sense of morality ('I never at any time approved of Christine's lust for black men'); true lurve ('I tell you that this funny little fat man meant more to me than any man in the world' — La Rach); and rank-pulling ('Half the office girls who titter when they read about me have had just as many affairs. The only difference is that I have tasted life when all they have tasted is the back seat of a car or a corner of the office behind the filing cabinet' — MIAOW!).

You have to hand it to little Mandy, with her puppy fat and

her collection of chins; she had a *chutzpah* that is rare in daughters of Albion. She was born to be a nice, pushy Jewish girl; can it be a coincidence that the end of her decade found her an Israeli citizen with an Israeli baby, taking tea with Mrs Moshe Dayan and giving teasing tonics to the troops between their battles against the camel-fuckers? Yes, probably.

In the Fifties Simon Dee was a failed actor — in the Seventies and Eighties he was an ex-bus conductor (thoroughly in character, he was sacked for swearing at his passengers) only getting into the news for being on the dole. His golden years, from first pirate radio DJ to networked prime time chat show host and household face, coincided exactly with the span of the Sixties, and *this* is no coincidence.

He had that flashy veneer and those empty depths, he had that smirking misanthropy and that peculiarly Sixties attitude that because people recognised your face they deserved the benefit of what was in your head, no matter what amount of banal garbage your brain was stuffed with. Glib sincerity, Gumbie-narcissism, that constant push push push to God knows (no)where, the need to be up to date while abhorring change — this is what it took in the Sixties and, like a cache of O levels or a fistful of luncheon vouchers, Simon had them in abundance. And when the Sixties were just a memory, he was about as much use as a halibut out of H2O.

I don't actually remember *Dee Time* — I was too busy doing things with my Cindy and Ken dolls — but I do remember it being a big noise. And on the magnificently entertaining evidence of *The Simon Dee Book* the man was a supremely self-regarding pinhead intent on a career of crawling conceit. Television could have been invented for him. The captions alone are a treat — a picture of Cliff Richard mindlessly wriggling his meaty hips is accompanied by the legend 'Cliff Richard has a serious side' — but the book's *real* strength is its candied, candid hate!!!

Never before between two covers has one man expressed so much contempt for the human race. Forget Nietzche. Forget Swift. Get Dee. On working for Radio Caroline: 'It was fine and dandy for the listeners, cosy in their bungalows in Barnet. But it wasn't quite as swinging for us, plugging away three miles out on the briny.' On being a vacuum cleaner salesman: 'Charm and chat plays a big part. So it's lucky I never found much trouble in chatting up housewives. Actually, women are their own worst enemy. A little bit of flattery and they're ready to believe anything. Believe you me, it never ceased to make me laugh.' On people on their way to work: 'The faceless ones are on the march, folks, brawling with deadly purpose into the metropolis, eyes half closed, bodies slumped over the wheel while wonderful Radio One twitters cheerfully. People hate people right now.'

Well you certainly do, boy! On he slugs, wading through his fans, Finchley and the sore point of how to painlessly dump your old friends when you make it to Olympus-On-Lime-Grove. It would be surprising if a man so full of distaste for his fellow beings did not consider himself to have the makings of a great leader, and sure enough towards the back of the book we find Simon's own manifesto, a camp *Mein Kampf*. In his hysterical state of self-worship Dee actually drew up a ten-point guide to living ('The Dee Code') and had it sent out to members of his fan club asking them to sign a declaration that they wished to register as supporters of its principles. For God's sake! He was in the process of organising some kind of secret teenage army — is that wack, or is that *wack*?

Even in the frantically self-promoting Sixties the Dee Code raised eyebrows and drew flak. 'Drearily platitudinous' — *The Times*. 'Dee comes over as a cross between Confucius and Baden-Powell' — *The Mirror*. The thing is that it is literally *impossible* to imagine the most self-adoring post-Sixties celebrity — even *moi* — drawing up one of those designs for living; Dee's wretched folly says more in one sad page about the goldrush hysteria that surrounded the Sixties media, the immortality that the flimsiest of talking heads felt close to, than any amount of Bookerite breast-beating and pillow-biting could ever do.

David Frost was once called by Kitty Muggeridge 'the man who rose without trace', a handle that was pounced on with great relish by jealous, untelegenic highbrows envious of Mr Frost's televisual grace. I have always found it rather funny that such a woman felt it suitable to sit in haughty judgement on someone who has conducted at least one great television interview — with David Irving; actually it was the only good television interview I have ever seen anyone conduct with David Irving, the one wherein Mr Frost tore out pages of anti-semitic filth and brandished them in Mr Irving's stupid face — but never mind. The point is that it was the phrase which gave David Frost the slimy image as the epitome of the slippery Sixties operator, existing only in the glare of the TV lights (I read the idiot card therefore I *am*).

But it was Simon Dee who died the day his ratings fell, and his contract was cancelled, somewhere at the start of the stark Seventies, and it was Simon Dee to whom the ostentatiously harmless machine in every home became both wonder drug and life support machine. It was a general public execution: when the silent majority switched channels, they saw to it that Simon Dee was dead.

Working Class Neros

In 1978, Jackie Collins was the only author that my mother (over 21, a factory worker) and my best friend (under 21, a secretary) read.

Jackie said: *'She was thin and white. She dressed and went out. The people in the street disgusted her.'*

But he said, HE said: *'In the moonlight, after midnight, I see you silly people out looking for delight. Well I'm so HAPPY, I'm feeling so fine, I'm watching all the rubbish and wasting my time.'*

Like all children of the working class, Johnny was raised to aspire to the ad man's tawdry images of the Good Life, good for nothing but remembering the long parade of cabbage gadgets on a quiz show. When I watch a quiz show I get angry, and I just want to *force* the contestants into brainwashing, education, what you will camps, where they would be *forced* to learn the bare bones of general knowledge, just so quiz masters can't ridicule the working class on peak time TV every week. I want to teach them that Romeo's girlfriend was called JULIET, that the first name of the President of America is JIMMY, both questions recently flunked by *Mr And Mrs* contestants. I just want to stop the virtues that 'working class' used to stubbornly stand for drowning in a sea of digital clocks and apathy.

Johnny got angry. The difference was — the difference that made him The Greatest where most rock anger makes the owner look moronic and old — was that he wasn't angry AT his parents, he was angry FOR them.

Youth culture fashions make money for the rich eventually, but the frustrated, special prole child who dreamed it all gets the memory. For a magic moment, wealth and influence trail slack-jawed after the ragged trousered philanthropist, his eyes gleam because it's precious to avenge the way your parents ape the middle class, the way the people you're meant to respect are always kept five years behind, in the dark, unconscious that when they finally get their prawn cocktail and their foreign holiday they're the topic of some quality paper's cartoon chuckle.

So you let rich kids copy your clothes and kicks, and you don't feel so ashamed on your parents' behalf. *Their* children can set styles, too! Even if they do get shorn and sold to less acute working-class kids about a year later by the old and rich. Let them fight over your old skin!

I can care if I want to.

You probably think people who read Jackie Collins' books are stupid and a shade sheepish, but compared to the slapdash, shallow and facile standard of 'youth music' shoved out these days — from quasi-Mod spiritual impotence to Dury's jolly little lolly lists — her work is positively noble. Unlike everyone's records, her books tend to point out problems, suggest solutions and set examples. They tend to have more wit, style and craft than your average single, last for days instead of minutes and cost around the same.

Let us compare Jackie Collins, a popular novelist, with Jimmy Pursey, a popular singer. Both appeal to an aggressively working-class audience, both make Having A Good Time their *cause célèbre*, both churn it out fast. Yet Collins has more skill in her cleavage than Pursey has in both heads.

This paper (*New Musical Express*) emerges every week to de-trivialise and analyse rock, so why shouldn't I do the same for blockbuster paperbacks? This is a popular arts paper, not an arts cult magazine. And the fact is that more young people in this country own a Collins-conceived record (*The Stud, The World Is Full Of Married Men, The Bitch*) than they do a Sex Pistols one. Like it or not, Collins' disco films and accompanying soundtracks have captured the money and attention of more youth than, say, *Quadrophenia* could dream of. The disco compilations sold under her titles spend weeks in the charts, and feature, well, more stars than there are in the heavens. Blondie, Taste Of Honey, Gene Chandler, are attached, sell and are sold; the tortoise and the hare, the old folk grin gummily. Money makes money out of the young and the black. It makes the marketing of every other youth-aimed album look as hypocritical as the pontifications on Ireland that Vietnam-whipped America makes.

The blockbuster is the art form of now and of the future. It sells more than anything; it is an avenue easily entered by any kid with a typewriter and two braincells to rub together; it is occasionally patronised and massively ignored.

Women in particular are making a wagonload of money out of popular paperback fiction; Mme de Stael, an early bluestocking, said that women are the presiding spirits of modern literature, and inventors of its characteristic form, the novel; classical literature is masculine, extolling political or martial heroism, but modern literature concerns internal journeys, emotional discovery, the feminine correlative of masculine adventure . . .

God forbid that being upwardly mobile should make women into John ME ME ME Wayne bottled up! Thankfully, the ancient wisdom of the British public shrugged off the self-indulgent shower of early Seventies Yank mind-wanking (*Fear Of Flying, Zen And Etc, Cowgirls Get The Blues*), simply because we like books with stories, like we like songs with tunes. An unpretentious people.

The blockbuster/best seller is still slightly synonymous with Harold Robbins, a gross and *passé* practitioner of the form. He has written 14 books; he is irretrievably rich and time-warped (his books swim with women who are movie stars, but he has never featured one man who is a rock singer, though they make the kind of money he admires avidly. Maybe he reckons they're not as virile as Arabs and tycoons).

Robbins began writing in the Forties and flopped horribly until the 1961 *Carpetbaggers*. This is the biggest selling paperback ever — over ten million sold. It has two female pivots; one dies for her sins (having sex a lot), the other gets raped, becomes a call girl and ends the book as a nun.

34

His books are thick in more ways than one. They are without exception about successful men (i.e. they have a lot of money) who have sex with beautiful, sick in the head whores. The fact that he always acts concerned and 'let's get to the bottom of this interesting case' about his women makes him extra-sickening; they never whore around because they like sex or are rebellious, but because their father, brother or Santa Claus raped them as a young girl. No one's personality is ever of their own making or mistakes; he takes very much the cheap liberal view of the poor little psychopath having a harsh childhood, bless him.

He cannot conceive that girls might not want to sleep with their old dads, but his men are never mother-fixated (he himself is an orphan). He tends towards prologues in which he tries to be a sex-free storyteller, but always lapses into perfunctory fornication within the first chapter. He fouls himself, you feel; you feel that he thinks if only he could write a book without sex in it (like Marilyn Monroe fretted that playing sexy girls meant no one took her seriously) he would be respected as a serious author. He doesn't realise that the secret is not to ignore sex, but to write it without clichés. Clichés are at their most ugly and pathetic when used in the context of written sex. He hurries sex, but dare not drop it; it's his ticket.

Like a paper sailor, he has a different girl's face on the front of every book, hinting. If packaging was representative of content, he'd have a different, seductive boardroom table on them. We link up well with our working-class crass-culture here; those Temple Goddesses of banality, the *Sun* Page 3 girls, get best billing — Stefanie Marrian on *The Adventurers*, Nina Carter on *The Carpetbaggers*.

Blockbuster writers, like singers, have developed definite personality cults, and thus has Harold Robbins — old and plain — been heavily dropped by the Seventies media. A good thing too; his writing has no blood, no odour, no visions. He knows nothing about youth, fashion or sex, which is why his pulp is so beyond the pale to girls, and to men with a brain (surely a good quarter of them?). He has claimed that due to a back injury (never stopped Jack Kennedy) he has only ever participated in sex while prostrate.

The funniest male pretender to Robbins' rusty throne is Burt Hirschfeld, who in 1975 wrote *Aspen* to cash in on the Claudine Loget shot-the-ski-instructor scandal. In it, sadistic men have sex-by-numbers with helpless, textbook-orgasm women and dice daringly with the killer 'grass', tee hee. Like with a lot of writers who have nothing to be proud of, the copyright is under another name — the Simon Jesse Corporation. Judith Krantz's *Scruples*, on the other hand, belongs to her husband's production company. *Scruples* was 1978's blockbuster success story and Krantz's first book — she has just signed for a record million and half paperback rights for her second, not yet written. Ms Krantz, as her copyright shows, may be a career woman (she was a *Cosmopolitan* editor for years, and the book was previewed therein which probably helped flog a few) but she is not a feminist — maybe this is why her prose is so corny and stiff.

It is basically Mills and Boon romance-on-the-pill. Those sexually liberated, self-improving, empty-hearted glossies are as bad as the jam-and-jumpers mousewife rags — in which the heroine finally finds fulfilment in pregnancy and the only lesbian is ugly, lonely and nasty. I have long suspected *Cosmo* of being a bastion of bad sex therapy; always advising girls to get contracepted and sleep around yet forever recoiling at the thought of lesbianism. As if to illustrate my point, Irma Kurtz, another of their ageing swingers, just published her first book — how a liberal Jewish New York girl reporter falls in love with a handsome Ku Klux Klan boss. Marlon Brando should love the part.

Krantz so thinks she can storytell that she doesn't even bother to gossip — the *only thing this kind of writer is good for*. *Ritz* is a hundred times cheaper and more aesthetically pleasing, and at least keeps up to date on what brand names to drop. Krantz writes old and soulless; the occasional yucky bed scene, no flash or snazziness, and making up for it by flaunting the trappings of wealth. The plot concerns a rich woman who marries a sugar daddy and then a ridiculous strutting wop, and then opens a vulgar (some would say exclusive) department store. She is a most uninteresting heroine, existing no further than the designer labels in her clothes.

The funny thing about books built around showing off how modern one is, is that the status symbols change so fast. To *Scruples*, Chloe is THE designer, Woodward and Bernstein THE party guests, Margaux Hemingway THE beauty; by now it's at least Ralph Lauren, Fran Lebowitz, Mariel Hemingway. It certainly doesn't date classically, as have Jacqueline Susann's Sixties showbiz epics (that woman knows more about pills and their reasons than Mr Roche does). Incidentally, this is the ONLY book I have ever read that features not one working-class person, not even made good.

It even sparked a clone in 1979; Michael French's *Abingdons, 'a simmering mixture of ambition, greed, betrayal and sex in the world's most glamourous department store'* — even the blurb has more art than the book. There are approximately four sex scenes to save face, so sketchy that the participants must be skeletons. The psychology of the mind that considers a place of buying and selling an aphrodisiac and an ideal setting for ecstatic sex is sweet and old-fashioned, but even this conviction he can't carry through, and the little passion there is, is reserved for heated discussions in the all-male boardroom. Poor sods trying to set swinging standards; Mullard in mink.

When the young use the blockbuster as a vehicle on which to peddle their art, they often do it brilliantly, tending as they do to know more about sex, fashion and extreme emotion, and not being bogged down with the nagging obsession of MONEY and BUSINESS — obsessions which quickly drain all the enjoyment from life.

The most vivid young blockbuster was written in 1959 by John Farris, then hardly out of his teens. As per usual with working-class-aimed fiction, the art-work (accommodating blonde in grubby slip, grappling) and the blurb (*'the co-ed where promiscuity runs unchecked and the curriculum includes sex and violence'*) collaborate to de-value the literature and despise the buyer — sell it short and sales rise, think the publishers evidently. Still, they can't stop *Harrison High* reading like a gritty *Grease*, a suburban *West Side Story*, a clean cut *Wanderers*; the beautiful writing seeps and sways like the best doo wop combo in the world, like Brian Wilson after Saturday night in his room.

The packaging of Harriet Frank's admirable *Single* (singularly graceless title) is misleading and maddening; *'Sexy . . . funny . . . moving . . . liberating, that's being single'* — God knows how *The Group* would be flogged if it wasn't in Penguin. *'Racy and raunchy . . . a sort of women's Harold Robbins'* said the stupid *Spectator*, not able to stray any further off the mark. It certainly isn't in the *'wild witty and winning tradition of Fear Of Flying'* — the universe as revolving around Erica Jong's clitoris, everything else in comparison, from the Holocaust to her husband, being transient and trashy, useful only for metaphors.

No, *Single* is like an urban Jane Austen novel, or Colette battling with the aesthetic unattractiveness of the IUD. Harriet Frank wrote the screenplay for *Hud, Conrack* and *The Long Hot Summer*, and like all the best writers she can see gestures and phrases as if on a screen while realising the wonderful way in which only the printed word lets language play. She also has a deep and realistic knowledge of America, poverty, the past, ambition, sex, success, the literary world and drugs — the book's junkie is a doctor and it is a little known fact that heroin addiction in this country and America was introduced by abuse within the medical practice, and that the first group of junkies were doctors, the morons.

Rona Jaffe's *The Last Chance* also follows the lives of four women; it makes practically every other book that has come out this decade look like a sick excuse. Jaffe is an old hand, too — she wrote *The Best Of Everything* in the Fifties — and her book is totally contemporary, totally classic. She has morals that make haloes look like L-plates. In accordance, the sex is rare but when it happens it's totally recognisable, real sex with fingers and moans. She's a woman who has savoured her surroundings, not just made a quick list of them between the boutique and the shrink. Her grasp of New York, of the agony and ecstasy of competing there, makes Woody Allen look like the wrung-out old stand-up he is.

All these books — the great, the good and the cretinous — are uniformly packaged in pretty girls and hyperbole to sell them to illiterate, crass, ogling Social Class Five. Jackie Collins sells her books on those two words — Jackie Collins — and what they stand for.

She is a famous figure now, more famous than Charlotte Bronte; she is the best-selling author in Britain, and a suitable case for critical praise.

There was a definite air of also-ranism over the Collins clique in the early Seventies, Jackie, the failed starlet and pulp writer; her husband Oscar Lerman, owner of Tramp disco where no one under thirty-five would be seen dead after George Best flew the nest; Joan the much-married, much-miscast elder-starlet of British films and her husband Ron Kass, resting after playing music-management musical-swivel-chairs for much of the Sixties (he has been President, Manager and various bossy things for, amongst others, Apple, Warner Brothers and MGM). Nothing sadder than glamour on the rocks.

Then BANG! it was like the Bee Gees — who dreamed THEY'D turn up again? In 1978, after the success of *Saturday Night Fever* and the renaissance of disco, the Collins clique went into a huddle and emerged triumphant with the film of the book of *The Stud*; written unnoticed by Jackie in 1971, starring Joan, set largely in Oscar's nightclub with Ron producing. What a jammy bunch; of course it ran and ran. The album got a gold watch when it finally dropped out of the charts, Joan Collins was voted the sexiest thing in the world, Jackie Collins became the new media authority on the Good Life; much prettier than Parkin or Cooper, and those film star connections.

Films had just boomed again, the compilation album was riding high; the Collins clique were perfectly suited to this new wave of vulgar frivolity. People who'd stopped buying books bought Jackie Collins because she was a mere unit of the latest glamour icon, buying the book became as un-cerebral and everyday as buying the record or seeing the film. She's responsible for starting a lot of people actually *reading words* again.

Though her productions are synonymous with Sex, it is probably her connections, her sister and her beauty which have caused this — she shows a great deal of marvellous cleavage on certain book covers, and though in her forties looks like a particularly sleek 27-year-old. She denies her books are about sex, and indeed she is very naive and 'later, much later'. When she tries to be modern and frank it's embarrassing *('She could feel his maleness.' 'It was good. It was meaningful.')*. Still people buy her books because they associate her, as a celebrity, with superior sex to what you and I and our friends will ever have (Harold Robbins' *The Betsy* was advertised with the most arrogant piece of boasting ever: *'The Harold Robbins women . . . they do the things that you only dream of.'* The dream police know!), and because it's like dating a chaste girl who you know has had a sordid past; 'She's been holding out on me, but TONIGHT will be the one.'

When both Robbins and Collins want to hint that a man is super-potent, successful and jaded, they construct a scene in which he has had sex with two women in one bed — a bit strong, what? Both *The Pirate* and *Lovers and Gamblers* start exactly this way.

Ostensibly she stands for the same kind of writing as Robbins — butch men doing things to eager beavers — but she writes from a sensitive, realistic, essentially female angle. (Yes, women may not have it in them to be geniuses, as we're always being told, but if there isn't a female Michelangelo, there sure as hell isn't a male Mother Teresa of Calcutta. Women still pretty much have a monopoly on humane, civilised behaviour — I'm sure all you trendy boys and old men who worship at the feet of *The Deer Hunter* and *The Warriors* won't mind me saying that — you like to think of yourself as noble savages, don't you? Happy head-hunting, anyway.)

Unlike men, particularly men who write about women and sex, she *knows* about women; about rich women, who manipulate and enjoy young boys, or young sexy girls who manipulate powerful old sods. Robbins' girls sleep with men because men are just so damn desirable, every last one of them; Collins' girls do it to protect and advance their careers, or to have orgasms. Countless male authors from St Paul to Hemingway to *Playboy* have been applauded for definitive comments on women's brains, emotions, sexual desires; can you imagine a white man daring to say 'This is how a black man thinks . . .' and being applauded by enlightened people? If men treated women like they treat blacks, it would be quite a giant step up for us. Collins never punishes her girls for having sex, either; her heroines without exception find one man they really want and end the book discussing film offers or going on honeymoons or simply in bed. Unlike male authors, she punishes people who ill-use others, not girls for having it away.

This year *The World Is Full Of Married Men* came out, with B actors and a star soundtrack which sold it to millions. The book was published in 1968, all wild models in bistros and neglected wives meeting sexy hippies at Ban the Bomb protests. The film happens in discotheques and throws in a pop star instead of a sexy hippie. The book contains some coarse, almost Chaucerian humour ('Ugh!' says the heroine after eating a canapé at a rival's wedding. 'A bit of dried up old sausage meat, sort of like the bridegroom.'), but it is most remarkable for its disclosure that Jackie Collins, a grown woman with a solid middle-class education, has — like the popular idea of the masses she deigns to give a glimpse of the Jet Set — little clue of where to use a comma, a colon or a full stop.

The World Is Full Of Married Men had some great disco on its soundtrack, but it didn't have Joan Collins in her underwear. Understanding that her sister is on a winning streak, Jackie Collins quickly cobbled together a sequel to *The Stud*, dropping the idiotic gigolo and concentrating on the character of Fontaine. *The Bitch* tries to move even more firmly into the youth market; the Olympic Runners appeared on *Top Of The Pops* singing the signature tune, and the soundtrack features Blondie, who is nothing if not loved above all else by the country's youth. The film consists of Joan Collins looking matronly, and failing badly to be wise-ass and witty to a sad bunch of B-men. With its classy and tempting TV ads, it will capture more young interest and money than you hope.

The book is slightly shoddy in its haste, but has its moments.

The heroine, thank God, is at last growing old gracefully (good God, if only musicians would learn to; a good number of them will be prospective grand-dads in a few years' time) and juggling young bimbos is becoming a bore — *'God! Was this what her life was all about? Fashion and Getting Fucked. Both were beginning to pall'* has more class than any number of rock songs about ennui. The book unfortunately features a male character whom Collins admires — a Greek gambler — and reveals an interesting flaw in her work; she cannot write well about men she admires, though she is excellent at ridiculing conceited, ugly and empty-headed ones. She writes about admirable men like an extra-florid Ian Fleming — incidentally, I have never read a writer who is so much in love with his creation as Fleming was with the appalling James Bond.

Both 160 pages slim, *The World Is Full Of Married Men* and *The Bitch* are blockbusters because they concern the sleazy side of wealth and show business, chase all round the world and sell brilliantly. *Lovers And Gamblers* is simply the archetype blockbuster of the Seventies, Jackie's *Ulysses*; published in 1977, 600 pages long, it is Collins' only foray into the rock world, though one can guess at many more now the record-buying youth have clutched her to their bosoms and put their money down her décolletage. In it Al King, *'rock/soul superstar and legendary Superstud'* has reached his peak at 37. Collins has described him as a hybrid of Presley, Tom Jones and Rod Stewart, a monster-birth befitting Roger Corman. The young, tough, gorgeous heroine is a mixture of Marji Wallace, Farrah F.M. and Everygirl who ever had a portfolio made up. The story concerns their careers and courtship; as storytelling it is beautifully and complexly constructed, skipping and hopping and flashing back and forth hypnotically. Collins seems to know the sordid side of rock quite well; there are good scenes of the drunk, uncaring star doing a lousy show to an audience who would rather stab out their eyes and cut off their ears than see and hear the awful truth, mumbling 'morons' as he is bundled into a car and taken back to the security of a sedative at the hotel, the crowd still going wild; the tragi-comic teenage toughs Plum and Glory who pool their savings, throw in their jobs and follow their star; Evan King, the son of Al, is simply the best adolescent study since Holden Caulfield, and the sullen dialogue between him and his father a work of trivia genius.

There is classy, incisive wit: *'Did Carol Cameron think of him as adequate? He thought not, remembering the compliments she had showered on him. "Enormous!" (untrue) "Never seen anything like it!" (unlikely) "You're the best!" (could be true, but with her track record probably not)'*. There is progression; by now Jackie has learned how to use punctuation. In fact she goes overboard. On full stops. And uses very. Short. Sentences.

Why I like Jackie Collins, and the new wave of populist, commercial, 'women's books' blockbusters in general, is that she strikes a healthy, often stylish and funny balance; between the tough gang of Boy's Own buddy-buddy war-mongers (carving out one's Nietzche at the expense of every other living creature that happens to be sharing your space, who've been making a comeback since America said five Hail Marys and forgot what a pathetic bunch of losers and bullies they acted like throughout the Sixties and early Seventies in Indo-China), and the godawful passive, put-upon, pessimistic 'feminist' 'self discovery' drivel that's still seeping out of America (thanks to Woody Allen giving self-indulgence and life-as-gauntlet-running a shot in the arm with his fashionable films) wherein women try to keep themselves 'open' and 'positive' just by letting men do what they like to them, and then look back on it and shake their head sadly over what a bunch of crap life is, but don't worry, I'll feel non-negative again when my new analyst tells me it would help me to relate to him if we had a physical inter-action relationship for five minutes before his next client arrives . . .

Jackie Collins' girls, and Rona Jaffe's, and Harriet Frank's, have the humanity and commonsense that male heroes tend to think it's prim and soppy to have these days, but they also go out and DO things, they don't sit around moaning and resigned to their raw deal. If she has ancestors in the arts, it's Forties film directors Douglas Sirk and George Cukor, themselves often dismissed for making 'Women's Films' (i.e. no one gets their head blown off in slow motion): the only directors who have repeatedly shown their female characters to DO instead of BE, who have focused consistently on the minds and ambitions of beautiful women as opposed to the ways they can be a help or a hindrance to men. They were populist, money-making artists who reached the masses in the way Jackie Collins does now.

Sirk was a genius, though, and Cukor was immensely talented, and Collins has at least ten years' hard practice in front of her before she even stops being that slight bit camp and throwaway; then she can start properly. Her main fault is that she takes for granted the idea that all working-class people want to live like the rich, and that this is a biological fact, that materialism is built into our brains.

Of course, many working people do yearn for nothing more than the crock of old crap at the end of *Sale Of The Century*, their lives DO run in ever decreasing circles around the Classified Results on a Saturday, and the reliance on a random lump sum obliterates any real ambition or hidden talent they may have, and may make them despise their class for not having a houseful of consumer status symbols; but this idea of material objects as *the* most important goal in life is the last Meaning Of Life that needs upholding, big business are the last people who need support. It's a shame that the books the working-class buy so much of encourage the Pools Lifestyle; fat comedians waving open bottles of Moet and dummy cheques at old people with hardly any teeth, John Conteh with his eye swollen closed presenting a cheque for £235,000 to a man with his tongue literally hanging out. *'IT'S FUN WHEN YOU'VE WON'* yells the glossy Pools Yearbook. *'SEE HOW EASY IT IS TO FILL IN A VERNON'S COUPON!'* The print emphasises the word EASY.

Still, Collins' morals are more all right than not. Her characters are allowed to take any kind of drug except heroin, have any kind of sex except rape and still settle down happily when they've tried enough. She believes in REVENGE and HAPPY ENDINGS — an impeccable, lonesome example to set against the misanthropic, back-pattingly-morbid, 'anything goes' fatalism of the majority of 'sensitive' books, films and rock music that gets taken so snootily seriously by the wallowing, trendy media.

I'm glad that so many people buy her books and make her rich; I'm sure that's a compliment she'll understand.

King Bunny

This is the story of a monumentally sexually unappetising man who started out at the age of twenty-six, married, frustrated, broke, walking the streets of foreign, expensive Chicago late·into the night, gazing up at the apartments above Lake Michigan and dreaming of the good life, and ended up less than thirty years later on an eight-foot revolving bed in a pleasure palace set in five acres of prime Holmby Hills that he never feels the need to leave, a bed from which he controls his crumbling empire by rising at five sharp every afternoon and holding business meetings in his dressing gown and slippers. In between he made a fortune from a sad case of mistaken identity; from the strangers men and women were to each other in the American Fifties, creatures from different planets. It is the story of an American Success; as triumphant, and as sad – be my witness, Presley, Ali, Marilyn — as that.

Russell Miller's *Bunny: The Real Story of Playboy* is brilliant, the best study of American success encapsulated in one sad shell-shocked shell since Albert Goldman's *Elvis*. Mr Miller gets in *close*; close enough to count the vibrators (4) on the Hefner headboard. He is as knowledgeable about exactly *why Playboy* was the first over-the-counter megabuck girlie magazine — because it showed girls you would be pleased to wake up with the morning after, not the smeared, smuggled motel skirt that was the norm; the Playmate was the girl next door to the advertising agency — as he is about the calamitous crack-up of the Playboy finances.

Mr Miller is sympathetic to feminist critiques of the Playboy mentality; and while feminist sympathies sit most charmingly upon a man, I would pay them less attention. I find it hard to see the wretched Bunny as a female Christ figure complete with floppy ears for a crown of thorns, crucified upon the cross of warped male fantasy. Being a Bunny was an easy route of escape from prole boredom for a stupid, pretty girl in much the same way as boxing still is for a young black man; but a Bunny, if she keeps her wits about her, can come out of it with her Securicor trinket *and* her self-respect, with no scars showing. The horror stories herein seem feeble and the wounds self-inflicted; the Bunnies were basically overpaid waitresses in silly costumes who got to go to a lot of parties, and through their own docility and fatalism performed various sexual acts which they did not enjoy with very rich slobs on throbbing waterbeds. But such *was* the docility and fatalism of these girls, that, had Hefner never invented the Playboy, they would hardly have become Congresswomen or fire-girls; rather, they would have found themselves performing the selfsame sexual acts without enjoyment for the pleasure of their meat-packer husbands in mobile homes in Montana. Bad sex in luxury is better than bad sex in debt. Against the Bunnies' right to choose to pander one has to balance *Playboy*'s (often financial) support of abortion rights and of ERA, and of the high mobility of female executives within the Playboy corporation.

No, the saddest thing about this great book is not the testimony of the virginal beauty queen from East Gnat's Ass who took a trip to the Playboy Mansion, got schtupped by La Hef (whose favourite sex — far be it from moi to gossip — is that preferred also by Polanski, de Sade and the entire male population of Argentina), and ended up hating herself in a booby hatch (from Bunny hatch to booby hatch, heh heh); the saddest strand is the showing of Mr Hefner, this physically disgusting, emotionally incontinent, dirty old (subhu)man as one who really considers himself a THINKER and a REFORMER, and actually does believe that all Playboy's tawdry little financial setbacks have been engineered by evil Right-wing cabals desperate to stop Hefner the Crusader from further enlightening the poor American people.

He is neither the Messiah he thinks he is nor the demon the feminists flatter him with, but yet another dumb millionaire, waited on hand, foot and cock, killing time; the greatest crime. The biggest evil he inflicted on the world he lived in was the Playboy mentality, the push-button theory of sex: you push the button and the bed comes out of the wall, you push the button and the girl comes. He confused SEX, that most elemental and uncontrollable of human emotions, with status, that most trifling and transient of human foibles, and he discovered too late that money cannot only not buy you love, it cannot even buy you good sex.

Lush Life

'Rosie Boycott is a well-known journalist. She is also a reformed alcoholic.' (That's odd — I thought she was a well-known alcoholic and a reformed journalist.) 'This is the story of how a nice girl like her made it from the top' — ? — 'to the bottom — and back again' — ? — 'during the wild and fragmented 1970s.' ! 'She was educated at Cheltenham Ladies College' — I'm impressed! — 'but soon found her way into London counterculture, experimenting with drugs, sex and booze' — that's enough! I'm shocked! — no, I really am!

When Miss Boycott was 21 she co-founded *Spare Rib* (which is about the one thing in her life she has a right to feel proud of, and doesn't), but she has also been a guru groupie, slept with camel-fuckers in Kuwait, chased John Steinbeck Junior around the opium dens and dives of Indo-China, been chucked in a Thai jail for toting dope across national borders (a real loss to the Brains Trust, this girl), and (swoon) sat on a sofa with Ava Gardner, a spiritual experience if ever there was one. She has also, I would bet my last litre of Bulgarian Bordeaux, read *Will There Really Be A Morning?*, the autobiography of Frances Farmer.

Miss Farmer was a shockingly beautiful, stirringly talented film actress of the Thirties who, ostensibly due to her drink problem, was committed by her mother for eleven years in State insane asylums where she was raped, starved and tortured in most ways known to consenting adults. Miss Boycott, on the other hand, is not beautiful, not apparently talented, and *was not even committed to an institution* — she merely volunteered to dry out in a private clinic on the King's Road where the inmates could even nip out to the Chelsea Potter for a quick one if it all got too much. (On checking into this netherworld Miss Boycott observes, 'The single bed was narrow, the wardrobe functional and ugly' — oh God, an ugly wardrobe! That's what I call pure hell!) Yet she still somehow miraculously feels that she has a tale worth telling. *Will There Really Be A Morning?* was such strong, sad stuff that it had the power to make you physically sick; the only physical response *A Nice Girl Like Me* will draw out of you is a yawn.

Frances Farmer completed her book days before her death from cancer, scornful of all the beauty and talent and celebrity she had ever possessed — none of her life had ever come anywhere near measuring up to her neurotically high standards. Miss Boycott has no such hang-ups — 'This book is not just about surviving, it's about thriving,' says La Rosie towards the end of the foreword, and that just about sets the self-satisfied tone of the tome. If this work is ever committed to cassette tape, God forbid, it will be punctuated by short bursts of 'My Way'.

To call it 'A story of the Seventies', for a start, is deceitful and misleading in the extreme (as well as being exaltingly self-important: as though it was the national Seventies norm to be a dypso deb); it is NOT a story of the Seventies but of the warmed-up Sixties leftover people — the Oxbridge dope dealers, the malicious demobbed limpets of the underground press, the big ugly babies who hung on in there well into the next decade, always with their safety nets slung around them; the family, the money, the old hippie boy network. Miss Boycott writes enthusiastically of her 1968 social debut, when all the sulky middle-class young were using the agony and upheaval of the real (Third) world as a sex aid — her first awareness of Vietnam gets one line, her first dope (drug and boy both) gets two pages. A caste of fringe media-filth thousands peoples this book; every disreputable hack who ever bored you silly in a corner of some tacky publishing party puts in an appearance here, fussing, fuming and fornicating themselves blue in the face.

Besides being horribly written, as though by someone whose first language is not English (the sex writing in particular is excruciatingly moon, June, Mills & Boon), the book is catty

('Next to me sat a fat, overbearing American woman, unmistakably lesbian' — MIAOW!), pretentious ('the Buddhist Alcoholic Group' — they haven't built the Pseud's Corner big enough for Miss Boycott yet) and smug (when Miss Boycott is not congratulating herself on being a gorgeous piece of ass, she is congratulating herself on being a gorgeous piece of assistant editor). It is only occasionally compulsive, in the way the worst of *Crossroads* is (will Rosie yield to the bottle today? Will she find true happiness with aristocratic Brian or A-rab Faisal? Neither, as if you cared; most of the successful sex in this book goes on between Miss Boycott and Miss Boycott's vibrator, hardly the earth-moving affair of the decade), and funny only once — the young Rosie, still on the up, editing feminist articles at home while her boyfriend bashes out think pieces with titles like 'Knickers Through The Ages' for tacky stroke magazines. Miss Boycott's faith in feminism seems always to have been a very half-hearted and shallow thing; she is basically, like many of the over-educated upper middle class, a Fixer, and she fixed off of feminism for a while the same way she went on to fix off of dope and drink of every description and is now probably fixing off of domesticity.

There are *so many* well-born wrecks around — their patron saint is surely Marianne Faithfull — absolutely *sure* that the world is holding its breath waiting to hear *their* story. The media is full of them and they're all the same, they all have the same story and they all believe they're blindingly unique. Certain people are *obsessed* with being SURVIVORS, and if there are no real hardships in their lives they will create their own obstacle course of a life out of anything that comes to hand. But this just doesn't work. Beauty on the skids, genius on the skids — these have their morbid fascination and their market. Mediocrity on the skids, or even mediocrity picking itself up, dusting itself down and starting all over again — this doesn't.

Food for Faith

A couple of weeks ago I went to a party at the Dorchester hotel, the launch of the *Official Foodie Handbook*, a celebration of gluttony masked in mockery. Three big cheeses in tall white hats had been bussed in at great expense to create the canapés, which starred marinated smoked salmon (two types), quails' eggs and the brains of calves. It was not quite the table of the Emperor Heliogabalus, who served the heads of 600 ostriches and conger eels fattened on Christians, but the thought that counted was fairly repellent, and sure enough I met no less than three people who were either on the verge of being inadvertently physically sick or who were actually *trying* to park a custard after eating something they had only identified after swallowing and didn't want to digest. This is the sort of thing that happens at pubescent cider parties, people reeling around throwing up, and this is also what happens when too much — infantile, regressive — attention is paid to food. This comedy of bad manners was crowned with a tragedy, the book coming out in exactly the same week as the Ethiopian story finally broke, a blight of bad publicity that the most vivacious of PR girls could not wave away easily. Marie Antoinette herself would have winced at the coincidence.

Then this week I saw the first TV adverts for a group called, if you please, Overeaters Anonymous: a hog in human dress diving into a fridge with a look of grief-stricken guilt on its face. It was clear that food was the temptress, the villain of the piece; an addictive evil on a par with drinking, smoking, gambling and glue, and that the poor fallen human had to be rescued from its clutches by this merciful band of saints. What next, I wonder? The picketing of patisseries as dens of iniquity, the routing out of bakers as pushers of wicked substances? Add up all the money and media attention paid to anorexia and bulimia, the slimming industry and the healthfood boom, and you might come to the conclusion that the obsession with what you shove into your face has gone too far. Food has been put on a pedestal, when all it should ever be put on is a plate.

I keep running across types of food I never knew existed, and people who use food for things I didn't know it could be used for; food as a *faith*, not fuel. In one instance, I left a celebrated nouvelle cuisine restaurant both penniless and starving — I expect one or the other from a restaurant, but not *both* — having eaten approximately one perfectly cooked carrot, three perfectly cooked peas, and a piece of perfectly cooked Scotch beef the size of a postage stamp. Of course, the appeal of nouvelle cuisine is that the sauces are all based on condensed milk, thus allowing sophisticates to eat baby food without revealing their true, insecure colours: you have to be both very rich and in the advanced stages of anorexia to properly appreciate nouvelle cuisine. In another instance, I found a loaf of bread in a macrobiotic household, *a bread with a beard* — such a handsome beard that it made the members of ZZ Top look clean-shaven. After fishing this thing out of its lair with a five-foot pole and driving a stake through its heart, I was scolded by its erstwhile owner, who said that the bread was best with its beard on.

Macropsychotic says it better; this same man, otherwise a paragon of elegance and tolerance, once seriously threatened the girl he had been married to for thirty years with *divorce* when he caught her eating an ice lolly; he was *serious*. There is something pagan, something gullible, something almost unbalanced about the amount of attention some people pay to food these days. It is the new god and the new drug; gluttons and macros are two sides of the same coin — one believes you can find a faith in food, the other believes you can find a kick. Both seek a tranquilliser, and both use food in a way it was never meant to be used.

Especially piggy and abnormal, I find, are those people who read obsessively about food, poring endlessly over cook books as though they were skin rags. After a certain age, drooling over pictures of food is as unbecoming as drooling over pictures of naked girls; messy. Food books are the new pornography. Lazy housewives through the ages have encouraged the development of a devotional mystique around the menial task of cooking, to the point that girls who serve convenience food (as opposed to inconvenience foods) to their guests, even when the food comes from the unsurpassable range of Mr Marks and Mr Spencer, the geniuses of the icebox, are thought to be lacking in manners and affection. Serving frozen food, even that which is perfectly free from preservatives, is still seen as a hostile act in some quarters. Lazy hippies smile snidely at career girls when they find out that the seafood pasta they have been guzzling for the past half hour comes from Marks rather than being the produce of more than one street market: you didn't spend three days chained to the stove? — ah, the decline of the West! Cooking is still seen as a way in which a woman proves her devotion — the longer it takes, the more she loves me; wear your burns like medals! I knew someone who married a beautiful, busy advertising girl with not much time for slaving over a hot wok; he described how his heart leapt one morning when he edged across the bed, buried his face in her hair and smelt . . . COOKING.

Food is there to keep you going, and what keeps you going best is what you like. Healthfood really has very little to do with health; America's oldest citizen, Charlie Smith of Florida, aged 136, has two shots of vodka for breakfast and a hamburger dipped in sugar for dinner. Western people use food as a drug; as a kick; as a tranquilliser; as a way to lose weight; as a way to purify the body. They cook to show love, or show off. In fact people in the West these days seem to cook and eat for every reason but one: *because they are hungry*.

Housewives' Choice

Just when you thought it was safe to go back into the job market . . . when you thought the Wages for Housework Campaign (surely the most anti-feminist crusade since the Cat and Mouse Suffragette imprisonment act of 1910: if a woman is being *paid* for housework, then a man has every right not to do so much as empty an ashtray — 'Not my job') and Mrs Thatcher's exhortations to women to get back into the kitchen and rejoice had all blown over, *Cosmopolitan* have struck a sinister blow in the undercover campaign to re-legitimise the housewife by abolishing their Working Woman Section on the entirely spurious grounds that 'All women work, whether they are at home or at Number 10 Downing Street'.

To confuse domestic chores with paid employment, and to say that they are separate but equal, is to take a step down a road paved with such sloppy thinking that the conclusions reached verge on the insane. To say 'All women work' is to say that there is no real difference between paid employment and housework. You may as well go on to say 'There is no unemployment in this country'; all the unemployed are capable of spinning out domestic drudgery from nine to five if they are so inclined, therefore they are 'working'. The point is that you either work or you don't work, you are in paid employment or you are not; housework is not real work, but on a par with washing the hair or the car, scene-setting as opposed to action, a preparation for living rather than a reason to live. That disappearing breed of beings who used to twitter apologetically about being 'just a housewife' had every right to apologise; the housewife is as treacherous a parody of the human female as the prostitute, and like the prostitute she can only exist in a society where men and women are strangers, and too scared to know each other.

Not only does she let the side down, but the housewife encourages men to behave badly. This country is as cut-throat and class-bound as it has ever been, and the thought of being poor, really poor, within it is horrifying — one is aware of the underclass in this country, and that it is possible in times of recession to slip right down through the scale and out into limbo, into the Underworld. For the weight and fear of social survival to fall only on the man, to make him solely responsible for the upkeep of another healthy adult human — as though his wife was a child, or an invalid — is to put on a man a strain so great that it may easily warp him. A *Ms* magazine report told of how young men felt jealousy and resentment when the young women they had married for their masculine vitality and virtues — ambition, competitiveness, hedonism — turned around and demanded the right to fold doilies all day; a report on male sexuality and the social control of women threw up its hands in horror at discovering that 'the average housewife' is being asked to do 'things' in bed that she was not asked to do ten years ago, and that she does not enjoy doing (in bed the housewife is at a terrible disadvantage; her role in life is, after all, to service her husband, to welcome him home from a hard day's grovelling into the clean and cosy padded cell where from five to nine he is king — her role is defined by his needs, and for her to veto any of them is grossly to overstep the mark). I have no idea what proportion of women who are slapped around by their husbands are in paid employment, but I would guess it is not many. There should be a caution on the marriage licence: being or keeping a housewife can seriously damage your health.

A young Oxford boy I know was seeing a teenage heiress, and during idle pillow talk about their futures she said, 'Oh, I just want to be a hicewife and have lots of children — and I want to have lots of divorces, too!' My friend diagnosed severe debauchment by *Dynasty*. My main objection to the housewife is not that she is a parasite or a collaborator — although of course she is these things — but that she is a mental magpie, attracted by anything with the sheen of sex-money that her own life so sorely lacks, and that her taste is making vast and nasty inroads into our precious popular culture. Housewives are a new leisured class; they do not earn the money they spend, and so they spend it more freely. They have their own subculture and patron saints; it is the housewife we have to blame for the slimy rise of Manilow and Iglesias, and for the success of Mills & Boon, and for turning station bookstalls into an ocean of slush. The housewife can skimp on food and spend her housekeeping like a sailor; somewhere some poor fool is eating horsemeat he thinks is sirloin steak, while his wife swoons to her new Julio LP.

And now the commercial TV controllers are saying that they see no point in ever buying another big budget feature film while you can make a sex-money mini-series — *Lace, Scruples, Princess Daisy* — for much less and be sure of hauling in a huge audience, at least 65 per cent of which will be housewives with housekeeping to spend. (The American showing of *Lace* beat out the first showing of *Star Wars* on another network.) It is the housewife, with her vapid, starved sponge of a mind, who creates the demand for this trash and drives the rest of us to distraction. To a healthy person, living a *life*, passion, ambition and megalomania are all in a day's work; to see lurid re-enactments of these very normal human qualities splashed all over the small screen every evening can get very tiring, like having your day played straight back at you, and it is the fault of the housewife, who experiences none of these things and needs her vicarious fix. (I can personally never understand what people mean when they call *Dallas* unrealistic; everyone dresses well and argues constantly, which seems to me about as realistic as you can get. I personally wish the networks would get with the re-runs of *Cathy Come Home* and *Poor Cow* so that I can indulge in a bit of hard-earned, much-needed escapism.) Housewives are the new Big Babies of our age, and every last marketing man is queueing up to throw his trashy distractions into her playpen. The housewives' choice has never been so pandered to, and popular culture has never been poorer.

Aunts in your Pants

What are the absolutely *worst* inventions of the post-war 20th century? I cannot give you the placings in reverse order, but I am sure of this much; somewhere, up there at the giddy heights of horridness along with the Tomahawk cruise and the boob tube, squats the Agony Aunt.

The anxiety industry has gone much too far. In recent weeks, I have read newspaper reports of primary school children calling the Samaritans, and of the anguish of certain silly individuals, who volunteered to air their dirty laundry on late night commercial TV sometime last year under the mothering, smothering eye of Mavis Nicholson. These silly people have since seen the troubles of which they sought to divest themselves worsen and worsen, and found that their neighbours regard them with horror, crossing the street upon sighting them — no doubt to escape further confessions. People are being encouraged to spill the beans/their guts too readily, too loudly these days, and the agony aunts are the guilty cheerleaders of this abhorrent trend.

Of course social tutors have always existed, and a good thing too: many of us still break out in hives when forced to approach copious cutlery. I knew a poor but honest pearl of a girl who was so upset by the array of good silver set out in front of her at her loaded boyfriend's parents' pad that she locked herself in the bathroom and climbed out through the window wearing two tons of taffeta rather than make a merkin of herself. She fractured her skull, but when I visited her in hospital she was pleased as punch that she had done the decent thing. 'At least I didn't show Nick up,' she crooned, hugging herself with glee. The boyfriend simply took her disappearing act as further proof of the tantalising shyness he had fancied her for in the first place, and they jumped the broomstick before her bandages were off. But she still swears he would have ditched her if she'd used the wrong knife.

So I am not pillorying Emily Post, or others of her ilk. But where is her ilk these days, who should be advising us upwardly mobile guttersnipes how to behave in polite company? The fact is that such agony aunts as exist these days (with the exception of the gracious, godlike Katie Boyle) are basically a Sex Thing; and like all public Sex Things, the agony aunt is a *bad thing*.

The first thing that is wrong with her is that she is only to be found in publications which are widely thought to be read solely by the working class — the condescending lady of the manor/ social worker connotations of this are nasty beyond belief. As if the middle class did not have sex problems! Why, everyone knows that the middle class *invented* sex problems!

Second, it is odd that the agony aunt is nearly always Jewish yet totally lacking in all those virtues which make the Jews literally the most indispensable race on earth; wit, spice, guts, wisdom. Their advice is always so bland and wet and passive.

Third, they are *not favoured*. Mother Nature was out on a picket line when the agony aunts got their turn at the cuteness counter. They are *plain*. I am not saying that ugly people should not *have* sex, but I do think that they should refrain from flaunting the fact, and from writing about it from experience. Sometimes, when I have eaten too much and wish not to gain weight, I do not stick my fingers down my throat like others of my coarse, sylphlike sorority but simply picture one of the country's leading agony aunts in the act of love. It never fails.

Fourth, they are obsessed with the Windsors. People who are obsessed with the Windsors are invariably sickening, but agony aunts being what they are are obsessed with Windsor Sex Things. Under the all-purpose guise of *caring* they make incredibly insinuating and smutty suggestions to the Windsors; Diana Drool, poor wretch, comes in for a cartload of clucking, smug chuckling and nudge-nudge advice whenever she complains of morning sickness, but it took the biscuit when Michael Fagan was surprised telling the Queen a bedtime story and it transpired that she and Mr Queen slept in separate bedrooms. The agony aunts broke out of their columns and ran riot with sickening front pages and editorials — GIVE HER A CUDDLE, PHIL! was one grotesquely familiar headline that will not leave my mind no matter how much ECT I subject myself to.

Fifth — and this is perhaps my strongest objection: I am turning into a little aesthete, I fear — they simply do not have the way with words to get to grips with love of the physical persuasion. They dare to venture into the empire of the senses, and *then* they turn coy and employ euphemisms; GIVE HER A CUDDLE, PHIL! I ask you! By 'a cuddle' they mean 'one' — GIVE HER ONE. Why don't they *say* so? Such giants amongst men of letters as Graham Greene and Norman Mailer have often made idiots of themselves when trying to write about *It*, and in their dotage they have tumbled this, and stopped; why then do these half-witted harpies persist?

There is just no excuse for them. If you need advice about lurve, and all the traumas that accompany its comings and goings, there are plenty of *proper* people you can get it from. Try the BPAS (British Pregnancy Advisory Service). Try a divorce lawyer. Try the Yellow Pages. Better still, try the Friend. You will recognise the Friend easily by the way it grabs you and wipes your eyes and by the way it does not tell you 'I regret I cannot answer your correspondence privately'.

Even better, you could always learn the ancient, much underrated art of Bottling It Up. There really is no problem on earth that strong drink and stubborn silence won't solve.

Idols on Parade

'Some people call me a teenage idol/Some people say they envy me/I guess they've got no way of knowing/How lonesome I can be.' (Ricky Nelson, 1962)

'Huge faces, bloated with cheap confectionery and smeared with chain-store make up . . . open sagging mouths and glazed eyes . . . when *I* was 16 my friends and I heard our first performance of Beethoven's Ninth Symphony. I can remember the excitement even today. We would not have wasted 30 seconds of our precious time on The Beatles and their ilk.' (Paul Johnson, 1964)

Of all the acts strutting their stuff in the rock and roll circus ring under the whip of the consumer-ringmaster, none falls further than the teen idol, and none so brave. We're not talking of incidental scream idols, from the Beatles to Bowie to Boy via dear dead Jim Morrison and Bryan Ferry, those glory glory days when every so often little girls and old men agree for a weekend on what constitutes 'real' music; *they* have the safety net of critical acclaim and the album-buying cognoscenti put by for when the screaming stops.

We're talking here of those young men judged solely by the arrangement of their eyes and mouth, that eternal triangle of adulation, those young men used therapeutically by young girls to transfer affection from their sweet-smelling girlfriends to the sawdust and sandpaper that adds up to your average adolescent boy – the soft skin shuffle — teen idols proper and pure, temple vestal virgins with spread-from-the-refrigerator smiles, those boys judged on their hair and teeth and bums, like girls or racehorses, judged and discarded like starlets.

The teen idol business has been an Equal Opportunities Employer for a long time — equally cruel and pragmatic, that is.

But the true mark of the real teen idol is that he is despised by all who are not working-class females under the age of 17, and despised most of all by the real 'rock' fans. Elvis Presley was despised by the outside, older world at large, but *his* fans quickly took over in the fear and loathing seats, cursing the letter sweater Frankies and Bobbies who were more to the taste of the *next* adolescents. The Beatles were the first pop crooners who refused to grow up gracefully and bow out to cabaret, and they cursed the world with a generation of senile adolescents, if not forever young then forever believing themselves to be, and forever pouring scorn on the musical tastes of anyone who actually *was*.

In the Sixties, innocent, I liked the Doors and the Beatles and the Kinks, and the Monkees and Herman's Hermits and Cupid's Inspiration and Vanity Fair and Love Affair. I didn't know that this wasn't allowed. I was amazed around the age of ten when I discovered that it was OK to like the first lot and dopey to like the latter, and I remember feeling distinctly persecuted by professional Rock Fans who somehow seemed to sniggeringly believe that every last girl who had a picture of Steve Ellis tacked to her wall was an infantile oaf, somehow non-U.

I took against pop snobbery *right then*, and I went off the Kinks and the Beatles almost overnight. I dropped my *Disc And Music Echo* like a hot pomme and wore my *Jackie* with redoubled pride. I was bent on a cultural life bereft of bull, and the basic, primal scream-and-sob lifestyle of the teenybopper seemed the best bet.

I was ten in 1970, and the geniuses of teenybop were coming round the mountain. Bliss was it in that very dawn, to be a mindless screaming moron . . .

In the first month of the first year of the Seventies, as befits the genesis of the muse of a decade's dancefloor, the most formidable infant prodigy since Mozart wrote his first symphony at the age of seven was unleashed on an unsuspecting planet. Little Michael Jackson, no more than ten, no less than perfection, 'I Want You Back'.

The Jackson Five were the first blacks to be real teen idols, to appeal to underage white girls almost exclusively; not like Frankie Lymon, who nobody knew was black until they saw his obituary pictures, not like the Supremes and Ronettes, who may have made white boys hot under the collar and white girls itch to dance, but who just *looked* like any other high yella doll with more easy money than dress sense through cold white girl eyes. And at Heathrow it was shown that teenage mass love knows no racial prejudice as the Jackson brothers were treated exactly the same as the Monkees had been, right down to precious Jackson hair being torn out and treasured.

Checking in at the same hotel on this same day were five brothers known as the Osmonds. They would not become known to British youth until 1972, when their hype would obliterate the heart of the Jacksons' art, but they were already big in their native America, and they were intent on following the Jacksons everywhere and getting down pat their every move. A *white* Jackson Five! — what more could a little girl ask for, *that* was the logic.

The Osmond Brothers had been appearing on networked American TV — *The Andy Williams Show*, no less — for five years previous to the Jackson reaction, to no recording avail whatsoever. But 'I Want You Back' had no sooner hit the top than the Osmonds were signed by MGM and rushed down to Muscle Shoals to record 'One Bad Apple', a No. 1 in dear dumb America and nothing here.

They were nothing but literally pale shadows of the Jackson Five with a few seedy, insipid, sinister quirks thrown in: their campaigning for the re-election of Nixon, their pair of deaf brothers who were kept inside the Mormon mansion sorting fanmail, the mother who was a cross between Tom Parker and J. Edgar Hoover, and that terrible combination of piety and naked greed that characterises the worst of family entertainers. Although the Jacksons were the official bearers of the Sound Of

Young America banner, it was the Osmonds who delivered the damaged goods.

Still, they became appallingly popular; from Donny's No. 1 with 'Puppy Love' in June 1972 to the Bros' No. 1 with 'Love Me For A Reason' in August 1974, the Osmond family chalked up *sixteen* Top Twenty British hits. A lot of their clout came from their sheer numbers; while only Michael Jackson (until Jermaine's tepid defection) had sufficient It to get out there and *sing*, the Osmonds — as the Osmonds proper, as Donny, as Marie, as Donny and Marie, and never forgetting the immortal Little Jimmy — had all bases covered.

Little Jimmy was exhumed every Christmas for the novelty hits, Marie's forte was cod country, the Osmonds as a whole did apocalyptic protest pop or white soul tearjerkers (Johnny Bristol worked with them, and did 'Love Me For A Reason' for them; I quite went for 'I Can't Stop' and 'Going Home', though I would rather have burned my silver platform boots than admit it), Donny and Marie wallowed in duets (tearful) while Prima Donny was *the* teen idol of the first half of the Seventies — all eyes, sob and slop. He couldn't open his yap without referring to his tender years; he had teeth like so many well-kept tombstones, and all the soul of one.

Donny Osmond seemed like teenybop's most traumatic moment until the Bay City Rollers hit the height in 1974. I remember a solid summer when there was no escape from 'Sha La La' or 'Shang-A-Lang' or 'Summer-love Sensation', from their moronic prancing and chanting, from their gormless unformed Pools-winner faces, from their tartan trimmings and short pants, echoed around me by the horrors I thought were my friends. I lost all my friends in the Bay City Rollers disaster of '74, it was like some plague, a complete wipe-out. They never had one good song. They couldn't scrape up one attractive feature between them. Yet girls went ape for them — I see echoes now in the lure of Manilow, and think there must be some theory for it, the Call Of The Mild, perhaps.

Anyway, my friends were solid gone, *ignoring* 'Red Dress', 'My Coo Ca Choo', 'Teenage Rampage', 'Always Yours', and *laughing* at the wise men and elders of the Seventies bop who

63

produced them — 'He's *old*. *And* fat. *And* a fairy.' A *fairy!* Just
because of a bit of glitter . . . couldn't they *see* the joke?

I wished in later years, when the *News Of The World* stories
came out, and the toyboys themselves kept trying to slash their
wrists in hotel bathrooms, that those Bay City Rollers fans who
killed my faith in teenkind were having a good sob in their nasty
council houses . . .

If the Bay City Rollers were the most objectionable teen idols of
the Seventies, and the Osmonds the biggest, and the Jacksons
the most talented, the most perfect was David Cassidy.

Alone, not *too* young (20 when he started playing the sweet
16-year-old Keith Partridge), with a beauty that depended not
on tartan or glitter or googly eyes, a boy with all the appeal of
the unholy trinity of Nymphet Fifties Susans — Susan 'Tuesday'
Weld, Susan Strasberg and Susan Lyon, all wide eyes and
wistfulness and wandlike bodies — whose scar held more allure
than Mrs Shirley Jones Partridge's fishnet legs or Miss Susan
Dey Partridge's mirage of a face.

But best of all, he had *angst*, that most essential ingredient of
the classico teen idol from Ricky Nelson to Nick Heyward. He
didn't flaunt or celebrate his youth or his clan; he had, as it
turned out, a supreme lonely starlet background, quite classy
and tragic. Until the age of three he lived with his mother's
parents in New Jersey — his parents, Jack Cassidy and Evelyn
Ward, were struggling chorines. When he was five, his father,
now big on Broadway, met 17-year-old Shirley Jones, fey
heroine of *Oklahoma!* That, as they say, was that.

From six to ten, his parents divorced, he was back with his
grandparents while his mother hoofed it for hard labour and his
father hoofed it for good. When he was ten his mother moved
him out to California, where his father and Shirley Jones
showed their heels in TV and films respectively. His mother
married the director Elliot Silverstein, who she divorced around
the time that David Cassidy finally came to like him. Jack
Cassidy and Shirley Jones moved back to New York, a castle in
Irving-On-Hudson, no less. After David achieved success his
father interviewed him on *The Merv Griffin Show* and asked him

if — sob — his parents' divorce had hurt him. 'Yes, it did,' said our hero, 'because I couldn't see my father as often as I would have liked.'

He grew up in Westwood, a suburb of Los Angeles, living a Tubes song. His adolescence was divorce, small showbiz, dull school, truancy, a transfer to a sinbin for affluent goofer-offers. His hobby was hanging around with the double-garage dropouts, throwing flour-bombs at passing cars. He was on the velvet road to nowhere when disease and salvation struck.

Born with deformed eye muscles which made him cross-eyed and embarrassed, corrective surgery blinded him at 12. He was kept doped on morphine and walked around in ludicrous diver's goggles for a month before the advent of The Eyes. Then there was a three-month bout of mononucleosis, during which he lay in bed thinking about himself. Apparently he changed, although his ill-health continued — ulcerous by 14, racked with agonising gallstones by 21.

He went to Rexford, the Beverly Hills school, where he had a black girlfriend. She came from South Los Angeles, near Watts, every day, and her parents had saved all their lives to buy her in amongst this rich white trash. From South Los Angeles to West Los Angeles is a long way in more ways than one; 'She was fantastic-looking. And, you know, she laughed a lot . . . and she was *already* bitter.' A campaigner for Bobby Kennedy, she took David to all-black campaign parties at which the K would be the only other white in the room . . . heady stuff for a Broadway brat. 'I felt a little uncomfortable, and at the same time I felt comfortable being where I was. I mean, the fact that I was white, and yet was accepted, made me feel really good.' His idols were Jimi Hendrix and B.B. King.

They dared to date for four months — a golden wedding in teenage terms. Then Martin Luther King was murdered and David Cassidy's best friend took up, quite reasonably, with a Black Powerite from Harvard.

He graduated in 1968 and two weeks later moved to New York, where he worked in the garment district, bothered the agents throughout his lunch hour and learned to sing at night. He quickly acquired quite a strong sweet voice, a manager,

65

Ruth Aarons, and a fast flop, 'Fig Leaves Are Falling'. But he *was* spotted by a Hollywood talent scout and taken back to the West Coast, where Universal liked him and cast him in lots of TV shows with a strong, semi-senile, central character and lots of gaps for fast young flesh to fill fresh each week; he walked on to *Ironsides, Marcus Welby M.D., Bonanza*.

In 1970 he tested for the lead as a singing eldest son in a pilot of a weekly teen entertainment, *The Partridge Family*, a half-hour romp through the lives of your average gorgeous, WASP, one-parent pop group, squeaky clean and filthy rich. He got it, of course, extra pathos being added by the fact that his own family life had been such a half-gone jigsaw, and that the home-wrecking ingénue who played his own brave single Mom had been the one who'd contributed to the mess in the first place.

The rest was hysteria. In the four years he worked on *The Partridge Family*, filming 26 episodes a year, he played some 350 shows in some 17 countries, made ten Partridge albums, eight solo albums and 17 mixed singles. He had to be smuggled into hotels in laundry baskets. Girls ripped apart limousines with bare hands at the merest hint he might be in them.

In London, May 1974, 800 fans were damaged in a crush, and one girl, 14-year-old Bernadette Whelan, died of a heart attack, a Disney Altamont as yet only rivalled by that Danish rape at a Kim Wilde show. Beauty does tend to bring out the beast in the best-behaved of teenies.

Such success is easy to mock, almost easier than failure, and rock commentators of the time didn't think twice about consigning him to the cultural trash heap along with Os Don, the Bay City Whorers and all. Well, they can never have watched *The Partridge Family*, which was always fast, sharp and funny and, once in a *bleu luna*, shockingly sensitive for such a frothy concoction.

They can never have seen his stage show, which was *something;* he was literally *thrown* onstage at running pace by a strongarm, and to dazed teenage eyes it seemed that he appeared out of nowhere. They can never have bought his records, which were perfection of their kind, which was uncontroversial, cherishable sob-pop.

He never made a happy record; whether breathing life into insistent originals like 'I Think I Love You', 'It's One Of Those Nights', 'Daydreamer' and 'Could It Be Forever' or giving the kiss of life to stale old Brill Building Brylcreem belters like 'Cherish', 'Walking In The Rain' and 'Looking Through The Eyes of Love' he was the most perfectly designed — by familial history *and* physiognomy — angsty young man yet. He hit the heights of his particular perfection in 1972 with 'How Can I Be Sure?', a banquet of sumptuous, scrumptious self-doubt — 'How can I be sure?/In a world that's constantly changing . . ./ HOW CAN I BE SURE?/Where I stand with YOU!' Aw, as Holden Caulfield would say, I wish you coulda been there — been 13, I mean.

The snipers obviously never devoured his regular writings in *Fab 208*, which were not the usual I-like-shy-girls-with-pretty-hands crooner cuckoldry (funny how the ones who expressed these preferences were months later revealed to have a soft spot for Irish stevedores with tattoos and calluses) but serious, stumbling explanations of WHY DAVID IS A VEGETARIAN! or DAVID ASKS: WHAT ARE WE DOING TO THE EARTH! What I didn't know about D.C.'s favourite dog 'Sheesh', his Irish setter 'Bullseye', his favourite long-haired black cat 'Boots' or his favourite friend 'Sam Hyman' by the time the Divine David stopped writing for *Fab* just wasn't worth knowing — I knew them better than my own parents.

He was earthy in a silky sort of way — the soft-focus dirty pictures in *Rolling Stone* (appendicitis scar and all), the dope revelations — in a time of sugar mice. And, probably most important, he was the most beautiful teen idol ever, before or since.

In 1975 *The Partridge Family*, which had made David Cassidy his first million before his 21st birthday, was axed without mercy when its ratings dropped. The rest of his twenties were the same kind of patchwork quilt of personal misfortune that his pre-idol life had been. He virtually disappeared from sight.

Shirley Jones divorced his father and married Marty Ingels,

who says of this time: 'David was eaten by success. He didn't know who he was. Shirley cried the whole time. No one who loved him could reach him.'

In 1976 his father, from whom by now he was totally estranged, died, drunk, in a fire in his Los Angeles apartment. In 1977 David Cassidy married the beautiful actress Kay Lenz, who looked like the third triplet in a triumvirate of Susan Dey and Mr Cassidy himself, and lived off his money and his love for a year or so.

But by 1978 he wanted to work again, and found attempts to get back before the camera harrowing; 'To the people who put you in TV and films it was like: "Who are you? Goodbye." I was yesterday's news. I felt a lot of pain about that, for having to almost apologise for having been a teen idol.' In 1981 his marriage dissolved.

If not for animals, his love of which had sometimes seemed a little *too* intense during his heyday, David Cassidy could have sunk without trace. As it was, the race meetings which he had been drawn to since 1973 became the only lynchpins of his life. He acquired his own red and white racing check, and his own runners at Hollywood Park. And he kept noticing a horse-breeder called Meryl Tanz, the kind of impossibly handsome red-haired divorcee that all callow young men believe waits somewhere for them.

They became engaged in 1982, and went into partnership breeding and racing some 60 thoroughbreds from a farm in Santa Barbara.

Horses, claims David Cassidy, are what pulled him through his teen idol years. They also pulled him *out* of the long hangover that his post-idol life was in danger of being and, by taking away the sour smell of desperation that hung around his late Seventies efforts to break into showbusiness, they have given him back his career.

Last year, at the age of 33, he finally starred on Broadway in the hit, albeit stinking musical *Joseph And The Amazing Technicolor Dreamcoat*, beating off Jimmy Osmond amongst others for the title role replacement of the delinquent Andy Gibb. He was a massive hit and deliriously happy.

68

At 34 he cut his first album since 1976 and married Meryl Tanz, a far better fate than that of Donny Osmond, last seen singing sub-standards to Miss Universe contestants in the evil Toy Republic of South Korea, and attempting to sue an English promoter when a British tour barely managed to fill the front rows.

Or of Jimmy Osmond, last seen playing a congenital idiot in *Fame* (typecasting?). Or of Michael Jackson, last seen conquering the world and going bonkers, well on the road to becoming the richest and also the most conspicuously neurotic black man ever to walk the face of the earth. In the way that the Motion Picture Academy awards a 'Special' Oscar to any old film star who makes it to 80, perhaps the music industry should award a Special Grammy to any teen idol who emerges from adolescent Olympus both solvent and sane.

The teen idol is the truest, the most honest, most useful type of crooner, really *used* and then put aside like a perfect but outplayed pop single. By the time you're 17 your life should not revolve around a revolving piece of plastic; that's just living your life in a playpen.

Yet followers of the God Pop find it *so hard* to tear themselves away, and invent new idols, non-scream, scowling idols, so as not to seem baby-wimps. Then they feel free to deride the happy idols of the very young like true sons of Paul Johnson.

Pop stars with ambitions to make money and make models didn't start with those shallow, Thatcherite, Devil's spawn Duran Duran, who are actually not fiends from hell but an attractive, unimportant little pop group with a knack for a tune; it's a tried and true path trodden since the days of the Beatles and the Rolling Stones, particularly enthusiastic practitioners of the sports and certainly never singled out as empty-headed moppets by the seers of Rock's Frat House. Far more *honesty*, if that is what you're sniffing after, can be found in Duran Duran, who want only what they appear to want, than in some supposedly ANGRY, ANXIOUS, ANGUISHED singing moron.

The Angry Crooner, the Thinking Crooner — what a

nonsense he is! As if one could be 'angry', and yet work in the profession of Liberace and Terry Wogan, the profession of Showing Off, every day of the week.

Angry people don't go into showbusiness, even if 'anger' is the flavour they are selling; anger doesn't speak the language of writing, recording, selling, time and time again. Bleating does, though, and if we look at the careers of the most outstanding of our Angry Crooners we may see that they are in fact nothing more than careers of bleating.

The difference between Duran Duran and Elvis Costello is that Duran Duran go out with models and enjoy it while Elvis Costello goes out with models and then hates himself and them for it, and then writes creepy songs complaining about it, making it 'respectable' in Rock Frat House terms. If it tastes nasty it must be good for you: *what* a waste of time.

The point is, and this should go towards helping the Rock Frat stop tilting at those tinted, blowdried windmills, that youth music has always been pushed and pulled between a mostly male (rock) mask and a mostly female (pop) mask.

Boys tend to like masculine American music and girls tend to like feminine British music, and the turn of girls' music always seems to be at the start towards the middle of a decade.

Thus boys liked Elvis — girls liked the Beatles. Boys liked guitar solos and heavy metal — girls liked the Bay City Rollers and Marc Bolan (Bruce Springsteen's resounding lack of commercial clout in Britain can probably be put down to the fact that he appeared on the market at the wrong end of the decade, in the midst of the clans of Osmond, Jackson and Partridge: Springsteen is perhaps as masculine and as American as a crooner can get, and perhaps the ultimate Boys' Musician, and it is interesting to see that the awful Meatloaf, nothing but a bloated, bastard copy of early Springsteen, cleaned up when he appeared at the *end* of the Seventies). Boys liked punks — but girls like Duran Duran, and there's no escaping them until around 1985.

Crooners today *like* looking clean and playing to female audiences; what's so suspect about that? Should they stink and sing to boys — should they all be like the Stranglers?

A lot of the antipathy is purely sexist and muddle-headed; quite why the sight of Duran Duran singing 'Is There Something I Should Know?' is considered insipid and wimpy while the Ronettes singing supremely submissive songs of lurve is some kind of work of art is beyond me.

The Rock Frat can't take the stuff that girl groups are made of when the people making it are male: Limahl singing songs about saving oneself (pace 'Love Child'), Wham singing songs about living at home and defying parents (see Shangri-Las), Nick Heyward singing about being loved and left and lonesome (Heyward is an interesting case for analysis; starting off with a certain amount of Rock Frat Cred, then losing it like a torn off stripe when the screaming started — as if it changed anything!), Paul Young specialising in yearning bovinity.

Girls on this landscape tend to be tough – like Bananarama, the Dion And The Belmonts of the Eighties with their sweet, swaggering boasts and persuasions. While that toppermost of the poppermost idol of young men, Tracie, tells them in one hot waxing that she'd like to KICK THEM REALLY HARD, ROAST THEM ON A SPIT and CUT OPEN THEIR HEARTS. Is that tough, or is that TUFF?

The mouthpiece for this generation of real fans is the lovely *Smash Hits*, the only music magazine ever to speak for the young female working-class who make up the majority of people who love and consume music in this country rather than a tiny minority of spiritual sixth-form boys who talk a lot and tape a lot and sneer a lot.

These girls are so broadminded that their king of kings is no dumb hunk but a soul-singing transvestite who sends a good proportion of their parents into seizures. Both they and their magazine are constantly mocked by the Rock Frat, and really, what is the point? Pop is a bauble, a streamer, a tickertape: serious feelings should be spent on serious things — to use serious anger in pop/on pop is debilitating, distracting, destructive. One could almost believe that the first protest song was a CIA conspiracy.

Every pop phase lasts as long as it needs to to grow its lovers up — there are too many people around too old to scream, and angry at the fact.

There are too many Paul Johnsons hanging out in the Rock Frat House, bitching about trashy fans, screaming at rubbish bands. Next time you get angry, why not hold back from stamping on the Duran Duran fan's fingers? Why not, um, go out and change the world or something?

Revolutions per Minute

One of the things that distinguishes pop music from culture proper is, unlike culture proper, that the exponents of pop culture are on average less intelligent than its adherents. Though often agreeable to look at, pop stars rarely have more than room temperature IQs, and we're talking cold rooms. In the majority of cases this doesn't matter at all — you don't have to be particularly bright to dress up in the latest letterati, make sure your teeth stay white and churn out the occasional platitude about love. Le Bon may not be an Einstein, but he's got his physics in all the right places. Provided they don't attempt to pass comment on anything other than their wealth and beauty, and don't pretend that their world-views extend beyond the scope of a Lionel Ritchie song, everything's dandy.

It is when they start preaching that the problems start. It is acutely embarrassing when a pop reporter solicits the opinion of any given crooner on things like nuclear war, the miners' strike and the Latvian Bestiality Reform Bill of 1908; this is the equivalent of asking a politician what he thinks about pop music, and just as cuddly Neil Kinnock will say something inane about the Beatles, so the pop star will say something equally banal and unenlightening about current affairs.

Even more suprising are those who actually condemn the music business (and remember, the accent has always been on *business*, not *music*) for not nurturing more pop combos purporting to have things to say about war and peace, who criticise the chart for being so un-UN. Sade is criticised for not being *black* enough, if you please; the idea being that because she happens to be black she ought to articulate the collective anxieties of other black people, and that her failure to do this somehow deprives her of any moral legitimacy. The trouble is that Sade is a singer, not a community spokesperson from Brixton. There's nothing wrong with articulating the needs and sufferings of the black community, and there's nothing wrong with Sade's cool jazz: why can't the two things be expressed by two different people? I have nothing against music and I have nothing against politics — but they can only be combined to the detriment of both.

The idea that by combining music and politics you involve a wider number of people in the political process, reach an audience who don't watch the news or read the papers, and generally ensure that the political problems touched upon by the music will be taken more seriously, is nonsense. There's no safer way to castrate a political view, to render it more harmless than to express it to the accompaniment of a throbbing backbeat; the horrors of nuclear war are made less, rather than more, tangible by expressing them in a form you can dance, sing and fuck to. When 'The War Game' was banned, when E. P. Thompson was prevented from giving the Dimbleby Lecture, when Bertrand Russell was jailed for participating in non-violent protest, the nuclear issue still had some *force*: in a year when Nena, Paul McCartney and Frankie Goes to Hollywood all got to the top riding on the nuclear wave, bombs are big, bland bucks. To describe 'Two Tribes' as the first 'protest' song since the Sixties, and to portray FGTH as somehow more 'genuine' than Wham! and Duran is a gross hypocrisy. In the age of 'The China Syndrome', 'The Day After' and 'Silkwood', Frankie may well get to Hollywood.

Stance bands place important ideas at the mercy of the vast and ruthless forces of fashion: it is all very well popularising a political view by coupling it with a megamix and proclaiming it in nice bold trendy letters on a T-shirt — but what is fashionable will sooner or later become *un*fashionable; to connect a political doctrine to a plethora of trendy paraphernalia is to portray it in the same superficial light as that paraphernalia; to reduce the decision about which way to vote to the same level of the decision over how long you should wear your hair.

So please don't feel guilty, all you clubbers and dancers,

about trotting the night away to a soundtrack of dynamic trivia. After all, you can always stay in on Sunday and get out that dusty copy of 'Kapital'. Just remember, when poring over those complex economic distinctions between real and surplus value, between base and superstructure, turn off the radio. Because whatever else it will do, it will not enhance either your concentration or your understanding of things which deserve your fullest attention.

The Rage is Beige

Look at the American singles chart; what do you see? You see
Stevie Wonder, with a dirge (un)worthy of Don McLean at
his most liquidised, you see Madonna, Prince, Hall and Oates,
Sheila E, Lionel Ritchie, the sisters Pointer and the brothers
Wham, the new bleached, blanched, blonde Heaven 17-helped
Tina Turner — you see a BEIGE chart. Beige: the colour of the
musical future. In five years' time there will be no black or white
music, no rock or soul; just Beigebeat.

From Moroder making Limahl and Oakey warmer (after
making Summer colder) to Rodgers making Duran danceable,
to Duran making Sister Sledge whiter by singing backup, to Pia
Zadora and Jermaine Jackson duetting in aid of the other's
sagging career, the mood is beige, a mingling of musical
pigmentation. What do the Police, the Style Council, Bronski
Beat, Animal Nightlife, Level 42, UB40 and Scritti Politti have in
common? Apart from the fact that they all probably loathe each
other, their world-view — and thus their sound — is grounded
in the belief that white rock is just too pallid to be palatable, and
that black echoes must be employed if the magic is to happen.
From the shambling reggae of some of the jazz vanities of
others, they are all one in the Beige Crusade. Sade is accused of
being 'too white', but this is as silly as calling Paul Young,
Hazell Dean or Helen Terry 'too black'; they are all simply part
of the Beige Generation.

Where did Beigemusic begin? Its roots are in Dusty Springfield
and David Bowie's cheesed-off cocaine soul, like most things; in
Blue Mink, the first unhip and unacceptable face of Beige
(Culture Club would later revive 'Melting Pot' as the Beige
Anthem, though); in K.C. and Hall & Oates. 'She's Gone', like

the later Beigeboom leaders 'Do You Really Want To Hurt Me'
and 'Young Guns', was played on black American radio
because the programmers assumed the artists were non-white;
the rise of the video was perhaps a sly way of letting the buyer
see what colour his favourite new band were. Beige found a
stilted, ill-suited manifesto with Two Tone and its feet with the
disco boom of the late Seventies, when even a band as hopeless
and white as the Rolling Stones went disco, and Beige faltered
and looked foolish on the cusp of the decades with August
Darnell and Bow Wow Wow (overt emphasis on sex sits badly
on Beige). But it has only really thrived and spread over the last
couple of years with the arrival of the second wave of post-punk
clubbers onto the pop market; those who, unlike the Spandau
Stranges, had their inheritance of black music untarnished by
playing at protest. Beige certainly didn't begin with Prince;
Warner Brothers spent five years and endless thousands trying
to break him, and only realised last year that the answer was to
take away his high camp soul falsetto, give him a guitar and a
Jimi Hendrix record, and sit back. (Michael Jackson, contrarily,
despite the nose job and the green contact lenses and the white
audiences, still sounds indelibly black, with all the throb and the
sob of olde worlde soul.)

No sooner did it seep out in 1982 that MTV had an unofficial
policy of non-black bias — 'Our interests are different.' As
though no white kid ever bought a Motown record! — than
Beigebeat went into overdrive, a spoke in the big wheels of
MTV's prejudice, a soul scrambler. Even those bands that didn't
SOUND beige, solid rock MTVUSA favourites like Big Country
and the Thompson Twins, had a — adopts South African accent
— *bleck* in the lineup. The boom of Boystown — women
singing for men, blacks singing for whites — took the meltdown
further. Talk of the Jazz and Torch-Blues Revival — part of the
Retreat From Rock scare of the early Eighties, popular with
displaced, disillusioned punks like Paul Weller, Alison Moyet
and Carmel McCourt — was also part of the Beiging of Britain,
and an easy way to dress well and influence people. A decade
ago, Working Week would have been dismissed by the hip as
bedsit whiners, what with their depressing ditties of faded love

and unmarried mothers; because of their protective Jazzbeige colouring they seem cool, even though it is obvious to the naked eye that they have much more in common with Cat Stevens than Count Basie.

Is it a shame, this thing called Beige? For white singers it is obviously a good deal; unadulterated white music is the weakest, most cringe-worthy art form on earth. And there isn't much to be said for black music proper; gospel, the music of religion, jazz, the music of drugs and reggae, the music of both, are all a dead end, the music of a depressed, oppressed people seeking solace on various levels from dark heroin cellars to mansions in the sky. Being a beige black is preferable to being a breakdancing black, one of the New Minstrels. Being beige makes good commercial sense; Jennifer Beals, *the* beige actress (black father, white mother) is a three-way winner, able to play Latins, pale blacks and suntanned whites. On the other hand, the Beigeview can lead to simplemindedness and bootstrap idealism; see *Fame* (small, not big screen). There is something sexually dulling about Beigedom: compare the treatment and toleration of Prince and Grace Jones as Sex Freaks, as opposed to the fear of Black Singers as Sex Threats in the pre-pop Fifties; compare the passive God-fearing sexuality of Donna Summer with the tarty predatory ethniCITY of Veronica Bennett; compare Eartha Kitt's old appeal — earthy kitten who made men stammer and straighten their ties — to her new position as cheap Boystown laugh.

Of course one doesn't want to hear black singers suffering, and one doesn't want to be separatist. But there was a time when there was Black pop, and it was good; the sound of Motown B.C. (Before California) not A.D. (After Detroit) was young and yearning, and thus it was the sound of the city. The sound of Prince and his Beige Brigade is the sound of the sex boutique in the shopping mall in the would-be swinging suburb; too clean for comfort.

The Hype Type

Poor Nancy Reagan — left with egg on her facelift. Still, that's the trouble with orphans — there's never one around when you need one. The 41 children from the People's Republic of Southwark that the First Toothpick took to London Zoo last week were orphans in the early afternoon of Friday; a few hours later they were not orphans at all. But if the CIA had been on the ball, they could have been (America is notoriously good at creating orphans). Appropriately enough, every move the Reagans made during the week that marked the anniversary of the D-Day landings gave quiet, dignified thanks for the defeat of Fritz — Fritz as in Mondale, that is, not Third Reich . . .

A publicity stunt is a press release made flesh and blood. Now, a press release is *not necessarily* a pack of lies — sometimes it is faith, hope and hyperbole. So it was *not really* a Big Lie when Bonzo's broad's publicity machine claimed she was taking a pack of 'underprivileged' small people to the zoo — her aides probably consider that all of those amongst us who have never been treated to a trip to the zoo with Nancy *are* underprivileged.

US presidents have always gone for publicity stunts in a big way — presidents and starlets, who have always had lots in common. Carter was not the only president who sought to use physical prowess as conclusive proof of his political virility (that disastrous sprint, when he ended up looking like the first dead man ever to cross a finishing line) — Gerald Ford was the worst, forever break dancing — or 'breaknecking', as he liked to call it — down every flight of stairs that crossed his merry path. When cute Samantha Fox had her fairly run-of-the-mill bosom insured recently she was following in Betty Grable's stiletto-heeled footsteps and executing a tried and true publicity stunt; by shelling out a few pence you can have your name bracketed with bigtime millions, and you can draw attention to the part of yourself that you consider your best bit — having a part of your body insured is tantamount to climbing to the top of the Empire State Building, ripping off your clothing and shouting 'OY! Look at this! Pretty good, eh?' (Working on this principle, Neil Kinnock will have his wife insured soon; she is surely the only outstanding asset this archetypal publicity-hunter has left.)

One of the best ways to get publicity is to associate with someone greater than yourself. In the grey days before he tied the knot, the panic-stricken Prince of Wales would be pursued endlessly through the pounding surf by wild colonial girls; not because they were driven insane with desire by the cut of his royal jib, but because the next day they would be splashed across the four corners of the tabloids.

These days the younger spiritual sisters of those girls are themselves chased along beaches by the younger brother of the heir apparent. Opinion is divided as to what he is after, but publicity probably comes quite low on the list.

The music business — née show business — is where you might expect the natural habitat of these Look-At-Me-World! antics to be situated, in which case you would be wrong. Like the Queen, who scuppered Mr Reagan's plans for a few snapshots of them picnicking on the lawn ('This is a private occasion,' she had to remind him, although she may as well have said it in Iranian as in our common, uncomprehending Anglo-American tongue: privacy is a pagan perversion to the American mind), pop stars do not have to run for re-election because they are completely powerless. The humble foot soldiers of the record industry do not covet publicity — it is thrust upon them by (fortuitous) circumstance.

The Sixties Archetype: P.J. Proby and the Case of the Split Trousers. P.J. Proby was one of Mother Nature's size 16s squeezed into a pair of wasp-waisted lederhosen. A publicity stunt was not the cause of his undoing — vanity was. Verdict: Not Guilty.

The Seventies Archetype: Bill Grundy v. the Sex Pistols. The lovable Spike-tops certainly swore on prime time TV — nobody is disputing that fact, Your Honour! But their bellicose *bons mots* were the result of churlish questioning and the conniving largesse of the hospitality room. Verdict: Media-Manipulation Not Proven.

The Eighties Archetype: The BBC v. 'Relax'. Prissy bonehead Mike Reid chose unilaterally to censor the debut disc of Frankie Goes to Hollywood when it stood at second place on the singles chart and in the heart of the nation's youth. The rest of Broadcasting House — in a disgusting display of senile servility — followed in their — tee hee — 'star's' wake. So 'Relax' was a sex song — so what? The last sexless record to get into the Top Forty was by the Singing Nun. Mr Reid banned 'Relax' when it was high in the charts. He could not have done more to ensure it reaching the hotspot if he had used up his entire expense account buying up every unsold copy of 'Relax' in the shops. Verdict: Frankie Goes To Hollywood Innocent.

The publicity stunt is almost solely the prerogative of the most important grown-ups in the world, the guardians of democracy — the politicians. (*Western* politicians — you do not see little Mr Chernenko doing the Lambeth Walk.) Witness grainy footage of the Beatles receiving an award from Harold 'My Constituency Is In Liverpool, You Know' Wilson, and YOU decide who was milking the occasion for all it was worth — Mop Tops or Right Honourable Member?

Amusing as it is to see politicians making pantomime horses of themselves, something about it sticks in the throat. And it is this. Politicians, like judges, like the police, like almost anyone you care to mention in a position of real power — they seem to have forgotten that they are not the country's masters, but its servants. And we seem to have forgotten that the hoops they jump through should not be of their own making, but of ours.

The Same Old Con

'The fact that I don't play anything and I don't sing is really funny. So I'm making a record and everyone else is doing the work. I take people off the street and throw them into a recording studio and come out with a record.' (Malcolm McLaren, counterjumper.)

Gaspo! Goshi! Does this man's daring and depravity know no bounds? One would think that Jesus had never . . . died for his sins! One would think there had never been a . . . Jonathan King!

Conspiracy theories are the opiate of the cocaine-Communists, and the pop arena has become a popular place in which to walk the dogma. The pop Svengali syndrome is central to this delusion, and when any blade raises his head and claims he is a pop Svengali, his word is taken for gospel, not gossip, and reams of newsprint bow down before him. I speak, of course, of Mr McLaren, and to a lesser extent of his Little Sir Echo Paul Morley, a blancmange in a McLaren mould made by McLaren-ex Trevor Horn, who has made the boy over in order to ensure that his tremendous talent gets the media attention it deserves — the lure of the loudmouth. Disregarding all the evidence (that the Electric Light Orchestra were using opera ten years ago to similar horrendous ends, that the gay ingredient is a tried and true moneyspinner (think of the success of the Village People, Goy Bourge and Cliff Richard, all B.F.), that Uncle Malcolm, in the last post-sex spurt of his career, has advocated SKIPPING, SQUARE DANCING and — sharp intake of breath — TAPING SONGS OFF THE RADIO — give 'em hell, Uncle! — as suitable leisure pastimes for young bloods: the Responsible Society could not fault him), there is an irritating consensus that

McMorley are ABOUT TO DO SOMETHING DANGEROUS. No one is sure of WHAT: but they are sure OF it.

So easy to believe, so *eager* to believe; some people like to believe that there are masterminds of pop, that it is a DIRTY BUSINESS as opposed to a big, benevolent Job Creation Scheme for the kiddies, the biggest, most benevolent one in existence. Spectators like the vicious vista because it makes them feel like amused and blameless victims (pre-destined failure/relax), and operators like it because it makes them feel like masters of the game. McMorley likes it more than anyone.

But they are *not* pop Svengalis, superhoned Spectoresque pop brains — Morley in particular is closer to being Frankie's head cheerleader; they have too many misses to be myths. What they are is souped-up pop scufflers — McLaren even has the office in Denmark Street, Tin Pan Alley — waiting for the big one, occupying roughly the same position as Jonathan King and Mickie Most held from around 1965 to 1975, yet scaled down (McLaren, with his curls and high-handed Hebraic condescension, even physically resembles the younger, thinner King). They will be remembered as lesser legends because they talk *so* much, *so* mindlessly — poor Morley has a big running sore in the middle of his face where his mouth should be — probably because they were never pop stars themselves, and thus never afforded the luxury of the eighteen-page Paul Morley interview through which to inflict their crackpot ideas upon a world waiting to melt in sheer molten awe. KingMost *were* pop stars, albeit in the Sixties and South Efrica respectively, and this gave them the freedom, having been big wheels, the freedom to be smooth quiet cogs. KingMost were BIG; they were as big as a poptrepreneur can get, which is bigger than his stable. One speaks of KingMost as entities, not as the ex-owner of Arrows or the ex-mentor of the Piglets; but McLaren is still referred to as 'ex-Sex Pistols manager', which annoys him but which he does little to deter, recycling old Rottenisms as he does ('I don't listen to music much. I don't like music much.' Come *on*, Uncle, you can do better than that), and Morley will never get past Frankie.

So what do McMorley actually DO? apart from talking a good (New) deal? *They have one hit novelty single approximately every six months after long and loud labours.* KingMost had a hit novelty single every three weeks — just the song, hold the manifesto — and what was so wonderful about them was that they *never* pretended to be important or, God forbid, *dangerous*; they knew that 'Leap Up And Down, Wave Your Knickers In The Air' would raise as many eyebrows and leave a world as unchanged as 'Relax' did. *Dangerous entertainment*: what a supreme de/conceit, so late in the day. The point is, do you believe we were put on earth to be *diverted* from our lives? Because that is ALL *all* entertainment does; it *diverts*, from 'Reflex' to 'Relax', from 'Madame Butterfly' to 'Elusive Butterfly Of Love' — the massage is the message. There is no such thing as *dangerous entertainment* — a delusion still held by many, and a delusion responsible for the acres of print strewn like palms at the feet of McMorley. Anti-establishment art is more likely to be a SUBSTITUTE for action rather than a spur to it; and *all* entertainment is an admission of defeat.

Better Cred Than Dead

So you want credibility? Well, credibility costs. And here's where you start paying — in eyestrain. Credibility is what media people have instead of A Levels and certificates for swimming their width. It is accumulated — and squandered — in many mysterious ways; it can be built on the very core of your soul or be the most cosmetic of paintjobs. But credibility has replaced paying one's dues as the official credentials needed before a career in the communications industry can get off the launch pad. When you are rich and famous you can do without it — though it hurts you so! — and once it has gone you will just have to live with the loss.

Like virginity or a contact lens, once you lose your credibility you won't get it back (at least not in this life.) And it can be mislaid so easily. Often people lose it through no fault or falter of their own but through a change of circumstance — Nicholas Heyward and the Wham chum chaps who started with a modest funky dose and lost it when their audiences became too young and too large for the boys in the biz to stomach. It is very easy to lose what little you have with one video and pay £££££ for the privilege; Duran Duran were not officially A JOKE until they started churning out their pitiable travelogues (excuse me, your Pools-winner mentality is showing).

It doesn't matter how much you've got, you can still lose/use it all; Frank Sinatra, with the once in a lifetime face and voice and name and fame, miraculously lost it all, and when hipsters talk about loving Frankie Sin they don't mean his recent stuff, his Godforsaken covers of 'Bright Eyes' and 'Just The Way You Are' — they mean they love the terminally slick ghost who crooned 'That Rainy Day'. From a credibility point of view

Sinatra is gone, dead, deceased — Dean Martin, paradoxically, still has his credibility completely intact: too pickled to disintegrate now.

The passion play of credibility were The Clash — crucified upon it. No one ever had It quite like The Clash and no one ever wasted it quite like them either, just frittering away those riches hanging around America (North, not Central!), wearing smoking jackets at airports, sniffing cocaine like scum — it was a terrible time for everybody. The Clash broke the collective heart of a generation, and they will never be forgiven for it.

It seemed impossible that Rotten could lose his, but he somehow pulled it off — got Fat, Went American, the two easiest ways to do it. But if he lost five stone overnight, made the greatest 45 in the history of the world and moved back to Finsbury Park tomorrow, things could never be the same.

As a crooner gets rich, it gets harder for him to keep his credibility, and though if he had to choose he would have the readies rather than the respect, it hurts his vanity that he can't *have it all*. He will do desperate things to get his credibility back, and may end up making a pantomime horse of himself — one thinks of Rod Stewart playing football in Beverly Hills or Keith Richard saying in 1977 'I could give these punks swearing lessons!'

Sometimes people who have had it for a very long time get completely drunk on it and believe they can get away with anything; witness perennial rebel darling Kenneth Everett casting his fate to the wind at that Nuremberg-On-Thames Tory rally. Overnight he lost all face with everyone over the age of 12, and acted impossibly hurt and disbelieving about the reaction. He had thought that he was literally credible past the point of no return.

There is no such point, although credibility can be a showbiz kid's insurance policy against follies committed in a previous lifetime — David Bowie survived an extraordinary, excruciatingly embarrassing skeleton in his closet — 'Where you from?' 'Gnome Man's Land!' indeed! — simply because he was *so* thin, *so* pale, *so* ambidextrous — in other words, he had incredible credibility. A lesser being, someone already overdrawn on his It account, would have been wiped off the face of the industry.

Nothing loses you credibility like outstaying your welcome and nothing ups your credibility like dying (suicide is rare, and has cachet, but murder is even better — by a) a nut or b) a jealous person. One gives martyr status, the other confers sexual success). However, there are other ways of winning and losing:

CREDIBILITY: SELECTED WAYS TO . . .

Get It/*Lose It*

- **Commit suicide**/*Threaten suicide*
- **Go to football**/*Go to bear-baiting*
- **Be cruel to people**/*Be cruel to animals*
- **If pop star, have children**/*If pop star, write sickening cutesy songs about children*
- **Be in jail**/*Be anyplace where that jerk who plays Brian Tilsley is. Or man escorting two girls (see Stringfellows)*
- **Have bad skin (signals Youth)**/*Be fat or bald (signals Age)*
- **Have scar, especially if divinely pretty (see Clare Grogan)**/*Have tattoo (coarsens the beauty and wonder of being a prole. The only good thing about a tattoo is the exotically livid scar it leaves when removed.)*
- **Marry a Jap or a German**/*Marry Britt Ekland*
- **If pop star, live with parents (if working class)**/*If pop star, live in America overmuch (see Clash)*
- **If pop star appeal to boys aged 20–30**/*If pop star appeal to girls aged 9–19*
- **Sneer**/*Smile*
- **Start a magazine with your own money and have it voted Magazine Of The Year after a few dozen issues**/*Start a magazine with your inheritance and go bankrupt after the first issue has been on the stands a few hours*
- **Sleep with AJP Taylor or Jaclyn Smith**/*Sleep with Al Haig or Lulu* (Torvill & Dean are an interesting crossover cred case: sleeping with *either* would be irredeemably bad while sleeping with both at once would do wonders for your reputation.)
- **Having boxed as a boy. Playing boxer in American film. Being a young boxer**/*Being an old boxer*

- **Having Italian or African blood/***Having Rhodesian or Manx blood*
- **If pop writer, fight for truth, justice and the socialist way/***If pop writer, fiddle expenses form and then sulk for entire afternoon when editor refuses to authorise payment*
- **Die gorily/***Live happily*
- **Pout/***If Welsh politician, romp in self-adoring way through Tracey Ullman videos*
- **Punch people/Give Pope Herpes/Defect or otherwise behave deceitfully towards Government/Sell out to gigantic multinational corporation/Act as apologist for worst excesses of Soviet Union/***Have anything to do (esp. sexually) with Radio One DJs (the only exception is Gavin Martin, who while being cousin to Mike Smith still retains his impeccable credentials)/Forfeit promising career on pop press to act as grinning monkey on a stick for fatuous commercial TV programme — or worse still as researcher for aforementioned grinning monkey on a stick/Compile sickening In Their Own Words rags while pretending to be valid human being/Write about pop music when you really want to be in band/Be in band but occasionally write badly about pop at fawning invitation of editor (an exception is Gary Kemp, who does it surprisingly well)*

You don't always know when you've got it. Look at Midge Ure — had it in Slik and thought he didn't. Didn't have it in Rich Kids and thought he did. Doesn't have it in Ultravox and thinks he does. One of the sweetest sights on earth is someone getting credible after 20 years of hard labour and mockery — one thinks of Tony Blackburn, who has *at last* been recognised as Britain's biggest and best promoter of black music over the past two decades. Think of Top Of The Pops, another one credible after 20 years of push and shove, 20 years of people pretending that it was a Fascist Friedmanite palliative, an old man's plaything, but now at last it stands revealed as what it is — broadly, the People's Choice. (Unlike, say, *The Tube* or the rest, which really are set-ups.) The only people who won't go on it are The Clash, who as we have seen don't matter any more. Whoever, man or beast, thought that they would see the day when Top Of The Pops had more credibility than The Clash! But that day is here.

Beyond those who achieve credibility, there are a) those who are born credible and b) those who have credibility thrust upon them:

a) Credibility can be kind. Considering that black people are allowed to get away with nothing whatsoever in the real world, it is nice that they are allowed every licence within the mysterious city limits of credibility. To be born black is in some way to be born perfect; but the road to blackness is a long one. Mr Rimbaud believed that there was an operation he could have to make him less of a pallid embarrassment, but people know better now and content themselves with employing black backing singers, inviting blacks into their pop bands, sleeping with them — *some* of it might rub off on you somewhere, leave you less painfully white. But you'll never have their *It*.

You can be a violent, mystic, drug-addled, stingy, money-mad, medallion-wearing moron (see Marvin Gaye) and still have It, if you're black. You can be a religion-ridden bigot — see Jesse Jackson and his cute 'Hymietown' crack: imagine the howls of liberal protest there would have been had a charismatic rabbi referred to Watts as 'Niggertown'! — and have It; black is absolutely the *only* colour a religion-ridden bigot can be and keep his credibility. Why, you can even be a sadistic ex-rent collector for Rachman who goes around killing girls and burying them in your back garden — but if you've got a black skin and a strategically-placed 'X' (see Michael De Freitas) the liberals will run around London like headless chickens giving their money and squawking up their petitions to save your worthless life. Which leads us neatly on to . . .

b) Credibility can be kinky. In recent years the violent criminal has found it easy to attain cachet. Though he should not be sex-violent (a strong moral note, so as not to offend the Sisters). He should have killed another criminal (oddly enough it is non-U to *inform* upon a fellow knave, but not to off him) or someone in a position of small power — a Securicor man, a night watchman, a bank teller. Then you start piling up the old

Open University certs; demure graduate girls with Oxford Firsts will turn to blushing jelly at the sight of your déclassé degrees. 'And you had to — SLOP OUT? And you shared a cell with — HOW MANY? And you haven't had a woman in — HOW LONG?' Cosh an oik and win yourself a bit of posh.

But no matter how criminal, or how black you are, there lurks a certain germ within all of us which, given rein, can rob you of every shred of cred. They call it MADNESS. The Kray twins lost their credibility not when their horrible crimes came to light but when one of them — I always forget which — was pronounced a fruitbat and moved from jail (U) to happy house (non-U). The most credible man in the world is oddly, a very rich pop star, one Michael Jackson; his blackness negates his square megastardom, and his enormous wealth is cancelled out by the fact that he hides away, he talks to the animals, he injures himself, *his money does not seem to have made him happy:* he is an honorary poor person. But his neuroses, which at the moment serve only to make him more interesting to the mandarins of cool, seem malignant, certain to run and run, and one day we will surely all wake up to find Michael Jackson has become the first mad black millionaire on earth, and a total embarrassment.

It is a long and winding road towards being worthy of belief, but that's credibility, the press release of your soul — gullible's travails.

Old Bores' Almanac

Greetings from Airstrip One, guys and dolls of Oceania! Now that 1984 has turned out to be *not* a totalitarian nightmare but a familiar friend, we can all afford to *relax* a little and look forward to what lies in store for the rest of '84. No omnipresent face glaring down from every wall (not unless you count Michael Jackson)! Still a few thrills available apart from Government gin! I'm all right! You're all right! We're all all right!

So let us look to the future with renewed hope as, hot off the presses from the Ministry Of Predictions, we peruse the news for the remainder of 1984 . . .

MAY

THE BBC BAN Julien Temple's video of the new Rolling Stones single 'Baby, Bite My Bum'. Comments a tight-lipped Mick Jagger, 'The song is about the delicate situation in the Middle East. Now nothing can save the world. Keith is inconsolable.'

FACTORY SUPREMO Tony Wilson announces that in future all gigs by Factory artistes will be known as 'rallies'. The Factory package tour plays Nuremberg, the bands appearing in Waffen SS uniforms. Comments Tony Wilson, 'The accusations of crypto-Fascism are simply facile. If those English *schweinhund* on the rock press can't see that this is valid social comment then I feel sorry for them.'

ONSTAGE AT A PACKED Madison Square Garden, Marc Almond stubs his toe on the microphone stand, bursts into tears and announces to the stunned crowd, 'I am quitting show business forever! Life is a sick joke! Everything is ruined!' Grown men weep openly in the streets.

DURING THE FILMING OF HER LATEST ART FILM *Mucky and Monstrous*, Deborah Harry hangs, draws and quarters herself. Better half Chris Stein comments, 'It was a valid cultural statement.'

FOLLOWING IN THE FOOTSTEPS OF ABC, Duran Duran make a political album entitled 'Mine's A Large Margarita, General Pinochet'. It goes platinum in eight days on both sides of the Atlantic. All proceeds from the album are donated to the band's hairdressers.

JUNE

FACTORY RECORDS INVADE Poland. Tony Wilson issues a statement to the press stating: 'Factory is an expanding operation and we simply had to have some lebensraum for our enlarged typing pool. We are building a label which will last a thousand years and, *Gott im Himmel*, it would be a bloody miracle if we didn't step on a few toes.'

MARC ALMOND'S comeback tour announced. Almond calls a press conference to declare: 'It's marvellous to be back! I feel totally refreshed! The press blew the whole thing up! It's a wonderful world!' Grown men weep openly in the street.

STING ALMOST DROWNS in a gold-plated jacuzzi full of Bollinger Brut. He gasps from his NHS hospital bed, 'I am still a Socialist.'

IN A SENSATIONAL article in the *News Of The World*, reprinted from *Christian Review*, Cliff Richard reveals, 'I have not had sex since 1961.'

JULY

CLIFF RICHARD explodes.

TONY WILSON takes poison in the bunker under his Manchester office. New Order flee the country for new lives in Paraguay with millions of pounds in uncashed royalty cheques.

STING'S MASERATI ploughs into a Right To Work march, injuring dozens of unemployed health workers. 'I am still a Socialist,' insists Sting through his lawyer.

DURAN DURAN become disillusioned with their newfound commitment. 'We are finished with politics,' they say in a statement to the press. 'We shall be voting SDP next election.'

Marvin Gaye arrested for the attempted murder of Paul Young.

AUGUST

Marvin Gaye jumps bail, strangles Paul Young in his hospital bed and surrenders to police.

The Times publishes a worldwide exclusive: *The Secret Diaries Of Tony Wilson*. Eminent historians are divided as to the authenticity of the diaries.

The Police play Sun City. Sting breaks off from counting his krugerrands to announce, 'I am still a Socialist.'

Rod Stewart is discovered in the Queen's bedroom. As he is led away Rod says, 'I still love Alana. Now I have to try and save our marriage.'

SEPTEMBER

Sting attends a party thrown by Heaven 17. 'I guess I'm not a Socialist any more,' he says, his voice breaking with emotion.

Marvin Gaye acquitted. 'Justifiable homicide,' Judge says, dismissing case.

Rod Stewart is discovered on a waterbed with fifteen Penthouse Pets. 'I still love Alana,' says Rod, 'now I have to try to save our marriage.'

OCTOBER

The entire troupe of the Dallas Cowboys cheerleaders bring paternity suit against Rod Stewart. 'I still love Alana,' Rod says, 'now I have to try to save our marriage.'

First annual Paul Young Convention at the ICA. Thousands sit at the feet of founder members of Q. Tips as they fondly recall Paul, known as the Berni Inn King to his disciples.

The BBC bans Julien Temple's video of the new Rolling Stones single, 'Everybody Suck Ma Thang'. Comments a distraught Mick Jagger, 'The song is about Belize. Or is it Grenada? Somewhere out there, man. Julien told me all about it. Now I can see no hope of resolving this issue peacefully.'

Elvis Costello beheads Scamp, his son's pet puppy dog.

When newspapers report the incident, Costello fumes 'How can the press be so callous as to do this to me? They have brought untold sorrow onto our happy home.'

NOVEMBER

PHIL COLLINS takes swimming holiday in Scotland. Sightings of Loch Ness Monster rocket to an all-time high.

PAUL YOUNG fans discover a vital clue in their campaign to prove their leader is not really dead. 'The line "*Come back and stay for good this time*," ' quotes a spokesman, 'clearly indicates that Paul is alive and well and waiting for the right moment to return.' Asked to comment on the rumour that Paul Young is alive but hideously disfigured, the spokesman snaps, 'He was born like that. What's your excuse?'

ADAM ANT performs his new single 'Round And Round The Garden (Like A Teddy Bear)' at the Royal Command Performance, and is introduced to the Queen Mother. He is immediately smitten. He tells the Sunday papers: 'She is my lovelight. This time it is the real thing! My whole being is in ecstasy! I only hope she feels the same way.'

SCIENTISTS INVESTIGATING reports of a huge black crater appearing in the Birmingham area call off their enquiries when they discover that it was only Kevin Rowlands yawning.

DECEMBER

ROGER MOORE is tragically drowned in an oil slick. His distraught widow Luisa says, 'I always told Roger to go steady with the Brylcreem. He just wouldn't listen.'

HOLLYWOOD is rocked by the news that in future James Bond will be played by David Bowie. 'The character of Bond will be rewritten for David,' says producer Cubby Broccoli. 'By making Bond a bisexual drug fiend, replacing his dinner jacket with a kimono, and making him a stranded alien recruited by the intelligence services, we hope to move the character firmly into the nineteen-seventies.'

A SNATCH SQUAD kidnap New Order from their castle in Paraguay and return them to the UK to stand trial for being boring little bastards. 'Ve vas just obeying orders,' one of them weeps in the dock. 'It vas all zat madman Vilson's idea.'

THE BBC BAN Julien Temple's video of the Queen's Christmas Speech. 'It was all about how the Commonwealth is one big happy family or something,' says Her Majesty. 'Now piss off.'

Soft Cells

The Home Office, with that typical Tory logic we all know and love, recently opined that the alleged 'short, sharp shock' regime currently inflicted upon young offenders is not working at all — and therefore the answer is to have more of it. Hooey! It is nothing less than *ludicrous* to toughen up these young thugs — they got into trouble in the first place courtesy of their hysterical masculinity, their total inability to weep at Douglas Sirk films.

Adult criminals are not subject to a never-ending Outward Bound course of mindless body-building; rather, they are encouraged to sit in their cells all day indulging themselves non-stop in the most mind-softening course of action known to man — studying for a sociology degree. While I would hesitate to suggest that this final cruelty, this terminal torture, be inflicted upon the soft pink brains of the young, I would suggest that the way to treat these young scamps is not to *toughen them up* but to *soften them up*. 'I was never the sort of boy who thought it was fun to go around beating up old ladies,' the glorious Marilyn has confessed, and it is plain to see why. He had too much respect for himself. Lesson: *A boy who has invested energy in his fingernails will not risk breaking one in the course of GBH.* There is nothing wrong with Britain's young offenders that a little bending of their genders will not cure. *Social consensus through cosmetics, lull through lipstick.*

Picture this: the boys' first taste of the soft life would come at their induction into the Soft Cell in the communal jacuzzi, wherein they receive their new institutional identities — *not* nasty brutalising numbers, but soppy Sixties names such as Gary and Steve were once prone to laughing themselves senseless at:

Tarquin and Jasper and Cosmo. The boys would spend the rest of the day memorising each other's new names and *touching*, a thing criminal class boys are notoriously loath to do — except when they are drunk, when they find it hard to keep their grubby paws off each other.

In the morning the boys would be awoken by the Hispanic husk of Julio Iglesias, crooning hot and heavy insinuations into their shell-likes. Naked, strapped to their pulsating waterbeds, unable to escape the aural attentions of Julio, they will know at last how it feels to be sexually harassed. Upon being released, there will be none of this nasty tough nonsense about cold showers and short backs and sides — rather the boys would take hot baths, liberally scented with the Mary Chess floral oil of their choice. They would wash their hair daily, skipping conditioner under penalty of the lash; the growing of hair would be heartily encouraged with financial incentives — say a fiver an inch. The boys would emerge from the bathroom pink and languid, in no fit state to mug a sloth.

They would then eat their breakfast. Pigmeat, which the criminal class takes great delight in gorging in the morning, would be banned ('Meat eating makes you violent. You won't find many vegetarians in prison' — Marie Helvin), as would boiled eggs, which must be treated in a violent manner in order to be consumed. A light *petit déjeuner* of muesli would commence. After breakfast the boys would take some exercise — *not* the brutalist Hitler Youth stomping around the compound currently encouraged, but rather an hour of aerobic dancing which would tighten up their bodies, loose from all those years of intravenous beer abuse, and help them towards what is surely the only goal of any normal, well-adjusted boy — to be attractive to girls. This aim would be furthered indoors, where the boys would strive to master the art of mixing the perfect dry martini, the adult equivalent of the Three Rs.

By now the boys would be ready for lunch: a little rice, eaten with chopsticks. Those big Bologna sausage fingers, so skilled in squeezing the throats of cringing OAPs, would come to know grief and humility as they struggled against the inscrutable, inviolate chopstick. The boys would be forced to carry on a

97

conversation as they ate; the savage criminal class practice of going at your chow in deadly silence would be discouraged by the discreet application of an electric cattle prod to uncommunicative eaters.

After lunch the boys would take short sweet naps on herbal pillows, awaking sweet-tempered and rosy-cheeked and raring to go and play frisbee. (Competitive sports, the greatest spur to young violence, would be completely outlawed.) In the late afternoon the boys would concentrate on their crafts — painting (though strictly water-colours — none of that dangerous free expression or modernism, Jackson Pollock being the biggest proof ever that vandalism pays), spinning, flower arranging, origami, learning and reciting the poems of Mr Wordsworth (they would be kept away from such poets as D. H. Lawrence and Ted Hughes, whose constant twitterings about violent death and manhood might easily inflame them. It is not difficult to imagine these young scamps finding in Mr Lawrence all the qualities of male bonding and throbbing fatalism that made them into football hooligans in the first place, and turning him into a substitute football team and busting a few heads in his name — *'One D. H. Lawrence! There's only one D. H. Lawrence!'*)

By now the boys would be exhausted. A light supper of artichoke hearts would be followed by brief visits by suitable guiding lights from the outside world — Norman St John Stevas, rather than the usual brawny dypso padre, for those boys wishing to take instruction in the ways of Roman Catholicism (as jailbirds often do), and Mr Quentin Crisp for those sceptics more interested in making a fast buck out of being a misfit than in finding salvation. And so to bed. And so the fragrant days and balmy nights pass by until our boys have paid their debt and grown their hair and are prised weeping through the gates of the Soft Cell, the most heavenly jail that ever stood, above the gates of which the motto is picked out in proud lurex against the silk scroll — BEAUTY THROUGH CRUELTY.

Genocide

Sayonara British Summer Time. Ours was a summer staged
for phantom Latin lovers who somehow never timed that
tango right. Lobo's Caribbean Disco and Geoffrey Deane's
abomination darted into the chart and August Darnell was left
with papaya on his face.

Don't knock the rock mi vida, and don't force the salsa. Go
and lie on a beach, maybe, until you can write one song as
effortlessly sunny, seductive and surefire as 'The Girl From
Ipanema' as sung by Astrid Gilberto (and The Girl is Marcia
Rodriguez . . .)

I'm pleased that the new Latin groove was just a two-hit
wonder because the whole colourful cascade seemed to poke
mindlessly vicious fun at and obscure what has been my
obsession for a good six years now. The state of Latin America.

Why? I don't know why. I have no connections. I admire
Barbara Carrera's looks. I was friends with a nice-natured
Venezuelan girl. I have a sneaking desire to own Herb Alpert
records.

Why? I don't know. It could be because Latin America, like
no other hot-spot on earth, sings out NAZIS AT WORK! Real ones
and spiritual heirs. And Nazis at work are my nightmare.

It's hell to be born on the continent regarded primarily as
Uncle Sam's backyard. You may be a republic with a ruler and
a parliament, you may be descended from one of the oldest
civilisations on earth, Aztec or Inca, but you know that while
Uncle's there you're just compost in his yard.

Uncle can take the worst people in your country, put
uniforms on them and give them guns and tell them they're the
guardians of Christianity, and they can kill as many of your

family, your village, your people as they wish.

The rest of the world may find out, but they'll lower their eyes because Uncle is a famous bully.

In Uncle Joe's backyard it's a different story. Uncle Sam, he say, in my backyard you can't be a democratic state. You can't be trusted. You want to be a COMMUNIST (for a country that professes to find Communism odious, America thinks that an awful lot of peasants are just dying to go Red at the first poss. op.). You must be killed.

And so every August Miranda cliché gushed about our flashing-eyed fiery Latin friends, all empty sensuous heads and roses between teeth, made real knowledge of this battered and bleeding continent ever more foreign. You'll go a long way before you'll find a rhumba skirt — bar Brazil, with its great window dressing. Vivid to visit, toxic to tell the truth in. You fly in — carnival. You fly out — carnage.

Brazil is not above a little night torture of anyone who commits the mortal sin of thinking. Brazil is larger than Australia and boasts the biggest gap between rich and poor in the world, riches to rival Houston and poverty to rival the Horn of Africa. Rags, not rhumba skirts, and not a reform in sight. Brazil, friend of the West.

The rest of the continent, embracing dozens of countries, varies — not as greatly as Europe, but then it is not allowed to.

There is parched, rural Peru, half the population of which is Indian. There is Argentina, with its celestial stairway of shopsoiled myths for the dazed populace to live on — Papa Peron, who wanted to be Hitler when he grew up, a Madonna blonde, the second home of Eichmann until 1960 when Israeli braves borrowed a British airplane and took Eichmann back to Eretz Yisrael to meet the hangman. Currently Argentina is the world's biggest exporter of meat. In their spare time, they enjoy applying electric shocks to Jews.

There is Paraguay, which has a history fetid with inter-Latin American wars; it seems to be a country encouraged and eager in the pursuit of money minted in blood. During the War the US gave the dictator Morinigo roads, cattle and airports to keep him sweet. After the War Paraguay became the most popular rest-home for Nazis. America never blinked.

There is Cuba, cute little island in the sun.

Only Cuba, under the protection of the Soviet Union, is allowed to chart its own destiny — the Red, and the rich, the oil-rich, Mexico and Venezuela, both bent on a programme of Latin American pride. Yes, we have no banana republics! Venezuela, particularly, has a democracy so solid that a handful of Communists regularly sit in Parliament.

But only the rich Latin Americans can expect to have their sovereignty respected. The rest may look to Chile as a taster of what to expect if they ever want to be their own people.

Chile's half a century of democracy was crushed like a cockroach in a Yankee kitchen when its people elected the warm, clever Marxist, Dr. Allende. The CIA had him killed and established Pinochet, dictator with a hand of pig iron who has run the country since 1975 along the God-fearing, anti-Communist lines of massacres in football stadiums, endless tortures and one-way car rides after dark.

This is the pattern in the backyard. And the UN says OK.

If Dante could see Latin America now he would shudder, especially for the small mountainous country of El Salvador — means Saviour Of Mankind — current intensive abattoir of the continent. Reagan is an older President than most, a more cowardly President than most, a stupider President than most, who must try harder than most to seem tough. Tough to American mannikins and hirelings means people who shoot a lot of people.

Having proved to be notoriously awful at *fighting* — America's war record is not to be believed — the USA goes in for murder in a big way. Is it yellow, is it brown? Is it infirm, is it an infant? Shoot it, shoot it! What are you, a coward, a Commie?

Practically all El Salvador's trade is with the USA and for 50 years the Salvadorean dictatorship — currently run by José Napoleon Duarte, who has himself had two fingers cut off by his own army, punishment for not being 'tough' enough — has been in thrall to Uncle. With the semi-success of the swashbuckling Sandinistas in nearby Nicaragua, the US got

101

scared and decreed a clampdown.

When will America learn that the way to stop people supporting Communism is to treat them well within the capitalist structure — not to kill them.

In two years Duarte's army, national guard and police force have murdered more than 20,000 Salvadoreans. They now average 60 killings per night and dump the bodies like garbage. Every morning children go out looking for the bodies of their brothers and sisters. There can be no protest. Debate ends with an American bullet in the head.

Duarte's goons kill to score high, to make up quotas, to look like big machines in front of their fellow goons, to feel American. There are over 230 documented cases of children under the age of 12 being killed by government militia. Children have been burned to death outside of high school gates. When the goons are in playful mood razor blades, decapitations and machetes ring the changes.

Phillip Jacobson, writing from the capital San Salvador, summed it up as 'ceaseless, random slaughter'. This state of affairs should have been made clear to America if not by the killing of foreigners by foreigners but by the rape and killing of three American missionary nuns by government militia earlier this year.

AND STILL, MASOCHISTICALLY AND MYOPICALLY, AMERICA CONTINUES TO SUPPLY THE JUNTA WITH ARMS TO THE VALUE OF AROUND 35 MILLION DOLLARS PER YEAR.

The UN called El Salvador 'a state of terror' and did damn all. Mexico and Venezuela have frowned. Sweden has tut-tutted.

Only in Germany has there been a decent show of anger — thousands of German youth went berserk with righteous wrath a while ago, all for a little country on the other side of the world, and the bombs are under the US bases still.

Why the Germans? Maybe they're the only ones close enough to Nazism to know that it wasn't wiped out, not in the 'democratic' West. It was allowed to seep away, to disperse and flourish in the guise of 'anti-Communism'.

Britain itself, God help us, bloodied its copybook forever

102

when, in August, Margaret Thatcher made a simpering gesture towards solidarity with Reagan by promising more than £1 million to the Duarte Junta.

It's sad to say, but those Germans — that's the kind of person who beat the Nazis in the War, not the apathetic, whingeing English who haven't raised a finger to protest this proposed atrocity, even after John Pilger bared it up the front of the *Daily Mirror* more than three months ago. This, now, in England, this is the closest we'll get to knowing that the concentration camps are being built and baptised . . . the knowledge, the powerlessness, the complicity, the futility of the VOTE. Don't it make you want to go to war, Joe?

'America's new Vietnam', El Salvador is being called by concerned liberals, but if only it was! Vietnam, though so long and large, was much less heartbreaking. There one was consoled by the fact that the Viet Cong were armed to the teeth by rich red friends, and at least one could feel cheered by the spectacle of the American army in action — winning their spurs in whoring, heroin and own-bombing.

The Salvadoreans are not rich in firepower. Worse still, no Americans save the score of Green Berets sent to train Duarte's dwarves have been shipped out, which means that no self-interested anti-war Second Front is simmering on the campus. Reagan simply pours in money he syphons off Welfare and that's that.

But it is Vietnam's worst moments on a massive scale. When America was in Vietnam the Pentagon began to spout racial theories along the lines of 'Asian' peoples valuing 'life' 'less' than Anglos. This was meant to lessen the impact that Mai Lai and similar massacres of entire villages of unarmed civilians would have on decent Europe — oh, these yellow people don't care about their babies and grandparents being bayoneted!

I swear, if there is one country that does not value human life and does nothing to prevent millions of its citizens from being needlessly killed each year, it is the USA — one life every 24 minutes gone with a gun, 200 children killed accidentally by the family gun last year. That's facts and figures about the cheapness of life in certain countries, not phoney rac(ist)ial lies.

103

Over 800,000 Salvadoreans have fled to the US for refuge, often after seeing blood relatives slaughtered. US Immigration has told them that there is no adequate proof of persecution — El Salvador not being a Communist country, no doubt — and delivers them to evil on El Avion Muerte. The Death Plane, in the tongue of the refugees.

Nazi is not a word I use lightly. When you decide that a person or a government is Nazi, then you admit that these people cannot be reformed, reasoned with or allowed civil rights. Nazis are for killing, pure and simple, and if you do less they go underground, multiply and kill thousands on the other side of the world next decade. To compare the Soviets to Nazis, as has been the rave amongst the cretin population of the world recently, is obscene and laughable.

When Russia bears a grievance she locks her enemies up in institutions for five years or so. I don't recall Russia ever making a dissident into a lampshade or a bar of soap. REMEMBER WHAT A NAZI IS.

Some people would have it that South Africa is a Nazi state; much as I loathe it, I think not. The slaughter is not conveyor belt but specific; when Biko is killed it's an outrage in the West, a headline, an atrocity that only supports what was already supposed — that the South African junta is a stupid and brutal minority suppressing a brave and deserving indigenous population through sheer force of white skin and capitalist clout. But the South African régime doesn't go out and cull the blacks every night.

There's something dangerously childlike about the rulers of Western Europe — they can't quite believe that a *soldier* in a *uniform* would go out and kill women and children for fun. If the Nazis should have taught us anything it's that psychopaths often wear the flag of their country.

When carnage becomes a manifesto, when the enemy is not the man with the opposing gun but anyone who doesn't wear your uniform, that's a Nazi. When slaughter is a spectator sport, like in El Salvador.

Imagine if over in France 60 to 200 people were being taken from their homes each night and murdered by a tiny Fascist

104

militia backed by American arms and alms. There are millions of Communists in France, after all. Maybe they make America nervous.

Would we let it happen? No, no! the French are . . . like us. Latin Americans . . . aren't. Another stereotypical lie, more slaughter tonight, as sure as you'll squeeze your toothpaste.

Thousands of young Germans know that there are no racial characteristics, just good people and rotten, and so they riot for their people, people too involved in the day to day business of making a living to care about Communism or capitalism or any other ism.

But for every political innocent slaughtered, some child grows up knowing about something called the USA which gives bad Salvadoreans the right to kill anything Salvadorean, even Archbishop Romero, the country's beloved religious leader, not like the people in the mountains who *defend*, and know about places like Cuba, Korea, Vietnam, Angola and Mozambique, where American machinery was amazed to find blacks and browns and yellows (with a little help from a different kind of white man, a white man whose money *arms* civilians, not *shoots* them) are *soldiers*, brave in a way that executioners and technicians can't win over.

I pity the Yank who still believes that God blesses America — he obviously hates the place — and I smile at the Party line which tells its people that God does not exist when he's obviously helped the ingrates to win every struggle they've taken up.

I feel admiration for those thousands of young Germans — they're the one indication to the Third World that non-Communist Europe, when it can be bothered to break out of the blindfold and blinkers, can be as brave, logical and decent as any helpful Communist commissar. They should serve as our example; if they can know that Fascism is THE evil and Communism is not, even though the Communists are just over the Wall and the Fascists are on another continent, then we have no excuse for our apathy.

Remember Vietnam and how every European capital inspired every American campus and MADE AMERICA STOP. Europe could do it again. Allies like the Germans and the slow-moving Swedes have made themselves known.

If we let the slaughter go on rather than incur Uncle's displeasure — well. The Germans have had a Nuremberg this century, and their youth are determined never to be tried as the Devil's tools. There will be a War Crimes tribunal in Latin America one day. I don't want to see my country in the dock as an accessory to atrocities.

Falklands: No Island is an Island

I write this on May Day so by the time you read this we will have won. When we have won we must go about the getting of wisdom; we will have taught a thoroughly intolerable bunch of Fascists a lesson and we must learn a few ourselves. Those tiny islands, those 1800 people, have acted as the most shattering catalyst that this paralysed island has experienced since Poland in 1939; never has so much been taught to so many by so few.

The Government will have to revise its amazingly stupid and cowardly nuclear 'defence' programme; the Government will have to change our policy of unrelieved support for Fascist juntas; the Left will have to learn that craven pacifism does not appeal at all to the proletariat; our old friends the Russians will have to learn that Nazi-nurturing is best left to the Americans; and the Americans, best of all, will have to learn that we, like Israel, their other foreign 'friend', cannot be controlled or manipulated as though we were some little offshore state, a Puerto Rico or a Hawaii.

With Vietnam and Iran fresh and festering in the national mind, America will have to face up to the fact that it has nothing to teach Britain about the art of war; on the contrary, it's about time they started sending their boys to Sandhurst. Like Israel, we have shown America that we will have a war with whoever attacks *us;* not just the people at whom the Americans point their silly little nuclear warheads.

The enemy are always interesting to look at under the microscope and dissect. We can trace right from the roots of Argentina the global inferiority complex that led them onto the Falkland Islands, that led them to raise their common-looking flag in front of Government House — but wouldn't you know it — the flagpole broke first time!

I'm afraid the Argies just aren't the Chosen People; we should have stopped, looked and listened to them a long time ago, the moment Uncle Sam informed us that they were one of our last bastions against Latin American Communism. We thought that the country's Fascism was a strength, but it was a weakness, the sort of weakness that always leads to overcompensation in the form of war.

From the time of the Spanish Empire, Argentina was considered a useless and dusty backyard — in this case to Peru, the precious metal jewel in the crown of Spain. By the nineteenth century Argentina had been abandoned and just lay there a-mouldering. Only Britain was decent enough to trade with the Godforsaken place — we even built their railroads.

Immigrants from Italy and France, Jews from Eastern Europe came to settle in the newly-civilised dustbowl. They brought few women, though, and in the early years of the century Argentina was already developing into the hotbed of hysteria and neurosis that we recognise today; there were 400,000 more men than women in a population of 20 million.

Buenos Aires became the centre of a flourishing white slave trade and men tangoed with each other in dance halls. Gosh! Nothing changes, does it?

Argentina more or less just messed along until in 1945 Juan Domingo Peron took power and bought back the railroads from the British in an effort to cobble together some kind of national identity. Argentina became rich from selling things to both sides fighting a war they took no part in; except afterwards, when they became a kind of Rest Home for Old Nazis.

It didn't last, though, as no régime founded on boasting can, and soon after his wife Evita, the shop-soiled Madonna of the masses, died Juan Peron was overthrown, in 1955.

He tried a comeback in 1973, but his new wife Isabelita could not live up to the advance publicity; 'She's no Evita,' people said to each other when she blessed them from the balcony of the Presidential Palace.

The fact was that no one could pull Argentina out of the pit it was in; at the beginning of the century Argentina and Canada had the same standard of living, but 70 years later the telephones didn't work and inflation reached 60 per cent per month.

A succession of military goons have been called in to repair Argentina's worsening ego, but all they have been able to do is borrow from the rich West; Argentina's national debt is much, much worse than poor maligned Communist Poland's.

The army became increasingly powerful, literally running the country; building steelworks and oil refineries, shipyards and airways. It wasn't enough for them though; not content with being the servants of the people, as a healthy army must be, they decided to make the people their slaves.

The Jews and Italians whose money held the country together have left this increasingly gory corner of the earth for Israel, Mexico and Uruguay. The armed forces, frustrated beyond belief at never having had the chance to fight a war, pitched into their own people; kidnapping children, torturing their parents, dropping liberals from helicopters; just plain old South American killing for profit and pleasure. There are now over 30,000 Desaparecidos.

The populace might have towed the line if the junta had delivered, kept the metaphorical trains running on time, but nothing was going right for Argentina. The hard man in the Palace was a jelly baby in the face of world recession with the worst economy in 50 years and unemployment of 12 per cent.

A few weeks before the invasion 13,000 people rioted in front of the Palace, the police retaliating with rubber bullets and tear gas. Just before that the junta agreed to elections soon on the incredibly guilt-ridden condition that there should be 'No war trials, no Nurembergs'.

Britain seems already to be forgetting that the war could have been stopped at this point, as the 'scrap metal merchants' planted the flag on South Georgia and the country crumbled on the mainland, if Mrs Thatcher had simply put her warships where her waffle is and scared the Argentinians back into internal mayhem, as the Labour Government had done before. The junta would have crumbled and the war would never have happened.

Instead she just sat back and continued to mouth off about the threat of world Communism while *La Prensa*, the most Anglophile of Argentinian newspapers, smirked that what Argentina needed to put it back in the pink was 'a nice little war'. Indeed, it went so far as to cite Government sources on January 31 saying that the Army were poised to invade the islands. Did Mrs Thatcher think that this was a nice little bit of black humour between friends?

Immediately the invasion was complete Argentina forgot its troubles. The Peron myth was restored, Galtieri appearing like a drunken Evita in drag on the balcony of the Presidential Palace while tens of thousands of duped peasants roared what translates roughly as 'President, we feel your greatness in the air!'

Meanwhile the Falkland Islanders were getting their first taste of Argentinian greatness. Rude gesture at a soldier — 30 days in jail. Disrespect to the flag — 60 days in jail. Islanders must wave white flags from their cars if they need help — white flags! The ghost of Hitler carrying out a little unfinished business. A radio ham said 'We are very alone.' The Argentinians offered to ship in cheap TV sets in time for the World Cup to show they were really all-round nice guys.

So it goes; one nation, warped and ruined by enforced trading and colonisation, tries to dish it out. There cannot be two pieces of land less capable of merging as one; Argentina the abattoir and the Falkland Islands with their lack of crime, their love of the radio, the way the only bakery in Port Stanley had to shut down because people are so self-sufficient.

The Islanders also happened to lose more men than any other part of the British Empire did, proportionally, and must have wondered if Mrs Thatcher had forgotten about that and just handed them over to her Argentinian buddies — the buddies she'd sold everything from missile destroyers to aircraft carriers, the buddies she sent Army experts to supervise the building of a destroyer which is able to track and destroy ships from 30 miles away.

While the Islanders were having such a terrible time, Britain really couldn't help seeming quite exhilarated by the whole thing. Apart from Mrs Thatcher, who was visibly upset that her Fascist friends had bitten the hand that armed them, there was something for everybody in the conflict. The Left could shout about Nazis and the Right could shout about having a lovely war.

But Mrs Thatcher could only stand there like an Aunt Sally with nothing to throw back at them. All she'd done when she heard that aircraft carriers, destroyers, landing craft, troop carriers and submarines were heading for Port Stanley was – you guessed it! — call up her Sugar Daddy and ask him to speak to that nasty Mr Galtieri.

Ronnie talked at Galtieri the Great for 50 minutes on the telephone and got the international rebuff 'Naff off', in essence. What is so funny about America is the way it cannot even persuade banana republics of its strength – imagine Russia letting a banana republic attack one of its friends!

The House was even more like a bear-garden than usual. Everyone was mad as hell and in high spirits — James Callaghan revealing how in 1977 when rumblings from Argentina were detected the Government had assembled ships stationed in the Caribbean, Gibraltar and the Med and stood them about 400 miles off the Falkland Islands, on the Argentine horizon.

Imagine how good the Islanders felt seeing that, and imagine how scared the Argentines were!

Keith Speed, the man of the moment, recalling how he was sacked by Thatcher for protesting against cuts in the Navy! (One great thing to come out of this conflict will be the total lack of credibility the nuclear white elephant will have from now. It didn't deter the Argentinians, where a huge Navy did.)

Michael Foot calling for a counter-invasion and being praised by Tory backbenchers for having 'spoken for England'!

Best of all was John Silkin, who spoke like a colossus. A Left-wing Jewish Churchill — why did no one think of it before? Perfect! The only flat note was struck by the Wet Left — Benn and Heffer and Hart haunting the Commons with the spirit of Neville Chamberlain. No matter how well-intentioned their

111

pacifist pleas were, in essence they were telling the Falklanders, 'Learn to love your friendly neighbourhood Fascist.'

On the streets things were just as hot. The 'animals' of Alf Ramsey's nightmares were a vivid and irresistible enemy. Brothers threw a tin of corned beef through the Argentine Embassy windows! Students were arrested for shouting 'Out, Fascists Out!' well into the night! Tesco banned Argie corned beef!

On the same farcical note, one wondered how British Fascists were coping with the crisis. When John Silkin spoke of the 'tinpot Fascist junta' they must have thought 'That sounds nice!' And then seeing people on the streets of Buenos Aires burning the Union Flag! One could visualise their little skin-heads exploding with the paradox, the divided loyalties of it all.

In the corridors of power the ritual sacrifice was made; doddering old duffer Peter Carrington, and while he was no hero he certainly shouldn't have been made to take the blame.

The invasion was a direct result of our being armed to fight the wrong war, our reliance on America and the Commie-baiting which made us blind to threats from other quarters — the very platform of Mrs Thatcher's foreign policy.

The Tory backbenchers were muttering about Munich — 'To be frank, it's been a balls-up,' said one — and at least 500 men on the erstwhile Task Force were going into battle with their redundancy notices in their pockets — great morale boosters. Thatcher and John Nott, her Commie-baiting caped crusader, should have been straight out on their ears.

But at least the Falkland Islands crisis will be looked back on as the time when the Tory Party decided that Thatcher was definitely the wrong man for the job. In the early days of the invasion the backbenchers realised with horror that Thatcherism was *not* Toryism and really had very little to do with it. As Mrs Thatcher didn't come through on law and order — Whitelaw is the first Home Secretary to *instruct* the judiciary to pass shorter sentences — so she has not come through on patriotism.

Thatcherism is not patriotism; it is a bid to become the latest State of the USA. As she set up secret talks with Haughey to give away Ulster because America does not approve of Britain's ties with Ulster, so she would have been quite prepared to give the Falkland Islands away had not she been pushed into a Pearl Harbour-type attack on her honour.

The most recent 'negotiations' with the Argentinians ended in February; negotiations imply that the challenging state has a right to the territory. 'Possession is nine tenths of the law' reverses when it comes to Margaret Thatcher's foreign policy — possession to her is an invitation for the highest bid. She wants to let all our 'Colonies' (Gibraltar, Ulster, the Falklands — though how a country can be a colony when the people of that country do not wish to be independent I do not know) go so that we can get on with the business, pure and simple, of being an American colony.

She is not a politician but a groupie; she should buy a one-way Pan Am ticket, a rah-rah skirt and a pompon and go and cheer Ronnie from the sidelines for the rest of her days.

There has never been a PM who has spoken so consistently in the language of confrontation as Thatcher. She wanted a confrontation over Afghanistan; she wanted a confrontation over Poland. She wanted to fight Communism, because since the war America has led us to believe that being a British patriot means being an anti-Communist, means siding with Fascism, if need be, against Communism.

Thatcher had swallowed this lie whole, and her inactivity in preventing the invasion was simply due to the fact that she was in a state of SHOCK. She had to fight the war against the Right that she'd wanted to fight against the LEFT. A poor girl's dreams, dashed!

Her and her Ronnie, at least, will have the consolation of going down hand in hand when the next elections come round. While the rest of the world acted so sweet — Europe and the Commonwealth and Japan imposing sanctions, the UN vote that Russia and China and Poland, our 'enemies', could have vetoed but abstained from — America did its regular impression of a dead sloth on the way to the dentist's.

Apparently, we and Argentina shared a common niche in America's heart! Uncle didn't want to see his best babies fighting! We can work it out — we're all against the Commies,

113

ain't we? Let's negotiate!

Thus began Al Haig's impersonations of a blue-assed fly. You bet America wanted us to negotiate; they must have felt sick at the prospect of us winning a war after all their recent humiliations in far away places with strange sounding names — Angola, Cuba, Korea, Vietnam, Cambodia, Iran, Mozambique. Let's face it, Americans make the most awful warriors; in fact the way the Argies have started shooting down their own planes reminds me very much of the funnier incidents of the Vietnam War, when stoned GIs would regularly napalm their own buddies. America can't stand the fact that Britain can win wars the old way, the honourable way, without dropping nuclear bombs or massacring Indo-Chinese grandmothers.

The Joe in the street, though, was looking at things very differently; he thought that Reagan was sort of *kinky*, not coming out in favour of an ancient democracy rather than a bloodthirsty dictatorship.

The sweetest messages were delivered to the British Embassy in Washington: 'God bless you', 'Come back safe', 'We're with you, boys'. Someone like me was shaken and stirred; American public opinion was more decent than I ever imagined it could be.

Could it be that the Washington policy of turning Central America into a slaughterhouse goes unprotested through ignorance and not callousness, as I had believed? I find it hard to believe that a people who loathe the Argentinian Fascists could possibly support the El Salvadorean Fascists.

But if the American people are getting better, their leaders are getting sicker. The night after the invasion America's United Nations Ambassador Jeane Kirkpatrick toasted Argentina at an Argie banquet. Mrs Kirkpatrick has to be a contender for the title of Sickest Woman In The World — she refused to meet a delegation of mothers of the Disappeared from Argentina, saying that they were Communist-sympathisers — and one fervently hopes that her career of evil will be one of the first casualties of the embarrassed American about-face.

We will come out of this healthier and more hopeful people — and we must use that strength to carve our future — not just leave it to dissolve into super-power dependence as we did after the last world war.

We must choose our own friends and our own enemies, not just take America's word for it, not just be America's bomb site. The Americans are the vandals of the world and want to make a trash heap of the world, like their own country is. For the first time in years, Fascist is a word of abuse even from the most Right-wing old Tory. We must build on those impeccable foundations. The blindfolds are off; the mould is broken in a way the SDP could not have imagined.

British patriotism means again, as it meant when we were at our best, stepping on Fascism wherever it raises its head, even in America's backyard. We will never again be eager to make friends with a Fascist; led by America, we've come to believe that being friendly with a Fascist strengthens you against Communists.

You cannot be friendly with a Fascist because he is by definition a madman; he will turn on you at any time, and he will turn on his friends first, as the Americans will find out.

How many more times will we arm ourselves against Communism only to have to fight Fascism at the eleventh hour? If we think Fascism is preferable to Communism, as Reagan and Thatcher have blatantly stated throughout their leaderships, then we are saying that the Second World War was a mistake and that we should have sided with Hitler to fight Stalin.

That is why Reagan and Thatcher are evil and dangerous, and that is why they should lose their jobs as surely as Leopaldo the Lush should lose his. They spit on the graves of the Allies every time they open their mouths.

This crisis will be a great breeding ground for a new patriotism, and there could not be a better nation to fight than Argentina, who represents the force for evil from the world's major countries. All the world's poison creation seems to have gone into building the cesspool up into a big strong boy for the past two decades; America feeds and waters them, Israel arms them to the teeth, Britain trains them, Russia spies for them and West Germany, the cretins, are helping them to build their very own Bomb.

Everything about them is pure filth, from the 30,000 Disappeared to the plans they have for the three million beautiful penguins who inhabit two sanctuary islands within the Falklands, owned by the Gloucestershire family of the late 'Penguin Millionaire' Leonard Hill, who loved and was obsessed by the birds. These beautiful, comical creatures, who cannot fly, are threatened by a company who have already been given the go-ahead by the junta to kill and boil them for human consumption.

How can barbarians like *these* be our Allies? Never.

We need to break away from all of them, the Super Powers and their goons, and we need to be alone, with a huge Navy and maybe even our own Bomb, like France and Yugoslavia. We should be no one's target, no one's door-mat. We deserve to be let alone and our people, wherever they live, deserve to be let alone.

It took America and Russia a long time to get into the fight against Fascism last time and it will be that way again.

Someone must stop them.

Nothing can stop us.

A Christmas Wish: The End of America

I refer to the misunderstanding of Soviet Russia as an aggressive
power, bent upon world domination — 'seeing,' to quote a
recent speech of the British Prime Minister, 'the rest of the world
as its rightful fiefdom'. How any rational person, viewing
objectively the history of the last 35 years, could entertain this
'international misunderstanding' challenges, if it does not defeat,
comprehension.

The notion has no basis in fact; it exists wholly in the realm of
imagination. While the United States has fought two major wars
in Asia and intervened with military force in Central America
and the Middle East, no Russian soldier stands today an inch
beyond where Russian soldiers stood in 1948, with the one
solitary exception that proves the rule — Afghanistan, where a
war is being fought with the same motives and the same
prospects of failure as it was twice fought by the British Empire
in India. If Russia is bent on world conquest, she has been
remarkably slothful and remarkably unsuccessful.

There are those who say that all this proves only how
successful the preventive measures of America have been.
When superstition is on the defensive, it will always resort to the
logic of the professor in the train who kept the elephants away
by throwing out bits of The Times and cited the absence of
elephants as proof of his success. This largest and most ominous
of all international misunderstandings is, like the others,
impervious to information or argument; but like the others it has
explanations for its existence and survival. Suppose that the
misunderstanding were by any chance cleared up; it is
impossible to compute the dislocation of the American
economy, industry and government that would ensue, so great

has become the degree of their dependence on it over the years.

The misunderstanding has also the function of sustaining a myth — the myth of the United States as 'the last, best hope of mankind'. St George and the Dragon is a poor show without a real dragon, the bigger and scarier the better, ideally with flames coming out of its mouth. The misunderstanding of Soviet Russia has become indispensable to the self-esteem of the American nation: he will not be regarded with benevolence who seeks to deprive them of it.

From a speech by Enoch Powell, MP for South Down, October 1983.

1983 was, as years go, a very good year. America is now well into its third bout of post-war insanity, and unlike the McCarthy years and the Vietnam years this new attack cannot be shaken off by discrediting a man, by losing a war, because this is the big one, the personality crisis that has been looking for them for two hundred and seven years, since the hour of their birth. After Grenada, Reagan's popularity has taken wing and the election of Fritzi Mondale or the Suburban Spaceman next year now seems unlikely.

America will never recover from the Reagan years. This year has seen the beginning of the end of America as anything but a geographical space — there's no ideal, no light of the world, no leader, no dream left. The mass hypnosis with which America has held the white world captive since 1945 is growing perilously thin and patchy. This year has seen the 'special relationship' at its most tepid temperature ever, and has gone the furthest towards destroying this supreme de(con)ceit which has always been the most malignant threat to post-war British sovereignty — castrated by a compliment!

With this in mind, I couldn't get too worked up about the little something Mr Reagan sent us for Christmas. There are countries all over Western Europe which belong to no one but themselves — France, Switzerland and particularly Austria, which shares borders with *three* Communist countries but shows no fear or desire for foreign weapons — and, 'undefended' or not, the Bolshevik jackboot is conspicuous by its absence. Of course it would have been nice, to say the least, if Britain had believed in itself enough to do as these countries have done, but never mind.

We *are*, in the eyes of the world, nothing more than another island protectorate of the USA, a cooler Hawaii, a richer Puerto Rico, populated by people who talk differently from Massah and have more colourful customs but never deviate politically from the mainland and have no opinions of their own whatsoever.

Taking this into consideration it is probably healthy for the weapons to stop here for a while; if the huge insult of Cruise doesn't put the average Briton's back up and make him vote in a government that will Return to Sender p.d.q. then this island doesn't deserve its independence — here's your red, white and blue grass skirt, *catch!*

Talk of islands and independence brings us limping onto the beaches of Grenada; it was truly pathetic to behold how *pleased* the Americans were to actually win what they considered was a war (albeit against 30 Cuban navvies) at last. Let's forget that they bombed mental hospitals and that half the troops killed were shot by their own side — this is the first war America has ever won, without Britain and Russia covering for it as they did in World Wars I and II, and after Vietnam, with more bombs dropped by the Americans on North Vietnam than were dropped by all countries during World War Two and *still* no victory, it is natural that the Americans are over the moon. A victory is a victory, even if you put Marvin Hagler in a ring with two crippled midgets.

There is just one thing that needs establishing when it comes to Grenada: either Latin America and the Caribbean BELONGS to the USA, in which case it is perfectly entitled, in the eyes of the world, to go in and do what it likes with the local government — or it DOESN'T belong to America, in which case America has as much right to invade IT as the USSR has to invade US.

If you care to look at your maps, children, you will find that WE are infinitely closer to Russia than Grenada is to America, and our circumstances are almost exactly the same — a country with a hostile political system and a huge stockpile of weapons masquerading as a tourist paradise — surely our nearest nervous superpower has a right to lay down the law?

It really is about time that people opened their eyes to the fact that, practically, logically, geographically, WE are in Russia's 'backyard', as America likes to divide things, and it really is very nice of them not to interfere with us — if only the US could learn a lesson and keep its filthy hands off Nicaragua. And don't give me that garbage about the Grenadians being 'pleased' to see the Americans — I know there were a bunch of grinning darkies, spiritual shoeshine boys, brought out to caper in the streets and say how glad they were to be under the thumb of Whitey once more. But people like to be televised; give ME a couple of days and I could easily pull together, say, 500 people in the wake of a Russian invasion who would gush and giggle and say how wonderful it was to be liberated at last by that darling boy Boris, and how the streets are safe to walk for the first time since the Charleston. It's all done, if not with mirrors then with TV cameras and scared civilians.

In the year when America had to apologise to France for whisking Klaus Barbie, the Butcher of Lyon, to safety simply because HE WAS AN ANTI-COMMUNIST (that he was also a Nazi and a mass murderer mattered not one whit, it seems) and in the year when America screamed itself hoarse telling Japan that they must arm, arm, ARM even as *Winds Of War* showed the Japanese Antichrist embarking on the destruction of America, the USA has never been more morally incontinent.

A 'Communist' country is now any which wants a little more from life than to be an American missile base/brothel/tourist trap — one and the same, aren't they? — whereas the 'Free World' is composed of countries who are anti-Communist: 'anti-Communist' is now the exact equation of 'Free' as the Americans use it, and thus the Free World contains such hotbeds of genocide as El Salvador, South Africa, Turkey and Pakistan. Phew — logic! There is no doubt at all that if Hitler was alive and kicking and living in the Third World today he would be armed, medalled and welcomed with all honours into the Free World Club — after all, the first people he put into the camps were the Communists. He can't have been *all* bad.

120

It matters not that in the Godless Communist world priests are not assassinated as they perform Mass, that nuns are not raped by soldiers and thrown dying into ditches, that whole villages are not wiped out by the army — words like 'evil' are reserved exclusively these days for Communist countries and usually used when a Polish miner has his toe stepped on. America hates Eastern Europe mostly because Eastern Europe is how Mr Middle-America believes his country once was and knows it can never be again — all white, fully employed, law-abiding, conformist. There could never be a Czechoslovak Charles Manson, or a Soviet Son Of Sam.

From the witches of Salem to the Evolutionists to the 'premature anti-Fascists' of Hollywood, America has always needed a scapegoat on which to pin its own singular poisons — viz. that it came into being as, to be brutal, the world's dustbin, there for all those who couldn't get anywhere in their own countries. In recent years America has realised that fastening on a local enemy weakens and divides a society, and has now pushed its frontiers of *internal* tolerance forward to such an extent that the Moonies, the mind-warping bogies of the Seventies, now hold a great deal of power in the White House and even own a Congressman or two. America's scapegoat is now the rest of the world, and its psychotic, neurotic foreign policy — America can have only enemies or banana republics, nothing in between — is its whole *raison d'être*.

There have been sick, corrupt, criminal, violent, poverty-ridden, ignorant societies before, and there are many now, all around the world. The difference is that Saudi Arabia or Haiti do not export their societies as role models for the rest of the world. Because the skins of America's leaders are white, it has managed to con a good deal of the world that it is a developed country, full of developed people. But America is not like any other country in the world, except perhaps South Africa, in that it is not a REAL country but a phoney state, based on genocide and built into a continent where it has no business. It does not hope for the normal things a real country does, whether it is Holland or Hungary, Belgium or Bulgaria — that it will get a little richer, a little more listened to at the UN next year.

121

America is one big Manson Family, misfits stuffed to bursting point with ignorance, hate and resentment, holed up in their huge ranch against the rest of the world, making the occasional marauding raid into the homes of the beautiful (from S. Tate to states of grace such as North Vietnam and Nicaragua) and killing them for the beauty and ease the thug outsider knows it can never have.

A cross between a playpen and a mental asylum, full of huge, unhinged children with a craving for sweet things and the capability to destroy the world, America is there. We cannot disinvent it, any more than we can disinvent herpes, or the Bomb, or snuff films, or any of the other remarkable gifts America has blessed us with. But America can be recognised — a place that has to rule the world to stop itself from feeling like an ashtray for the world's dog-ends — and it can be isolated — the amount of countries which agree with America about any given foreign policy target has never been smaller — and it can be admitted, at last, that America is not a country: it is an experiment that has gone terribly, terribly wrong.

Greeneland Revisited

Brighton, Haiti, London, Liberia and Mexico. Come with your courageous literary courier to Greeneland: where all people are one person — corrupted and cruel from cradle to grave — where every hope is a lost cause, where you will hear no birds sing and no sweet nothings, but just the one true sound — the sound of things — crusades, countries, marriages — falling apart. He who is not busy committing adultery is busy plotting espionage, in Greeneland. The coat of arms there has no brave boasts — no *Liberté, Egalité, Fraternité* — but something like *Isolation, Violence, Failure*.

Graham Greene: 'Human nature is not black and white, but black and grey.'

It remains one of the mysteries of the age that this excuse for a human being, this brantub of neuroses, is responsible for the most terrifyingly beautiful writing I have ever read.

He grew up to take tea with Ho Chi Minh and take sides with the Sandinistas, but he was born in 1904 and doomed to attend Berkhamsted, where his father was headmaster. All sensitive adolescents, capable of so much yet powerless to effect any real change in their lives, feel boredom more strongly than any other emotion, but it is something they tend to break out of when they break into the big world — a benign boredom, a skin that can be shed and kept dead. Greene's boredom was a rare strain — a malignant boredom that I believe he cultivated as an elegant escape from that ultimate horror to the sensitive young — *heartiness*, bearing down on him mercilessly in the shape of robust, ruddy, public school, Anglican normality.

'I was seventeen and terribly bored and in love with my sister's governess — one of those miserable, romantic loves of adolescence that set in many minds the idea that love and despair are inextricable and that successful love hardly deserves the name. At that age one may fall irrevocably in love with failure, and success of any kind loses half the savour before it is experienced.' (*The Lost Childhood*.)

Such non-specific angst is very teenage, very Tears For Fears, but the young Mr Greene did not leave it there. He ate bunches of deadly nightshade; he took a score of aspirin before swimming ('under the circumstances highly reasonable'). He discovered 'without any sense of strangeness' the gungame invented by White Russian officers who also thought that anything was better than boredom but abandoned it when the roulette routine with his brother's revolver became as banal as the aspirin aquajinks.

By now it must be clear to the modern reader that Mr Greene has always been *not quite right*; rather, he was a chronic depressive from a very early age. Depression is very near to being the norm for artistic types — from classicists like Eliot to brawlers like Mailer to sentimentalists like Betjeman to sensationalists like Fleming, all of whose world-views identify them immediately as depressives more unmistakeably than any scientific test. The modern recognition of depression as an illness, something that one can admit to and be medically treated for, must have robbed the world of many talents as well as creating many numbed inmates of institutions — if Greene was growing up today he would have had all his poisons and enchantments electric-shocked out of him by the age of 21. Instead, having evaded suicide he made the next logical step in the warped schedule of the depressive. At the age of 22 he was received into the Church of Pessimism, the Church of the Poison Mind — the Catholic Church.

Here was the terminus of the depressive's dream, here was the place where no one would tell you to snap out of it, pull your socks up, play the game and all the rest of that clear-eyed, optimistic, Anglican pep talk. Here Greene's feeling that everything was useless, worthless and hopeless was at last confirmed for him in the Church of original sin, Limbo, Confession and Purgatory; at last he must have felt that the transformation from boring English public schoolboy to ancient exotic beast was complete as he jumped into the jaws of the Old Faith and wallowed in the smell of the incense, the memory of the Inquisition, the total lack of logic — all the endless superstitions that Catholicism is founded on. You can accuse Catholicism of many things, but it certainly isn't *healthy* and it certainly isn't *hearty* — and those were the only things that the young Graham Greene really dreaded being called.

In case someone is about to accuse me of anti-Catholic prejudice, I suppose I may as well declare it myself right now. I am an atheist — thank God — but when anyone says 'Catholic' I become Martin Luther, Ian Paisley, every Orangeman who ever banged a defensive drum. My loathing is in no way racial or personal — I never met a lapsed Catholic I didn't like — but I do believe that it is very logical and very credible. And I must admit that I distrust, despise and hate Catholicism.

God knows that no religion has much to boast about; whatever its avowed purpose, religion usually ends up as nothing more than an excuse to make war and dispatch a thousand or so, a million or so souls from this world out into the great unknown: God as some insatiable cull-master. Perhaps only the Quakers escape, and their belief is too pure to be practical. The Eastern religions, thought by teenage heads since the Fifties to be in some way different and progressive, are very similar to the Western religions in that they still permit believers to act like complete scum — the Japanese were Buddhists, and Buddhism is painted in the West as the most pacifistic of religions, when they committed their terrible atrocities in the Thirties and Forties. (It strikes me that the Godless, i.e. Communist armies, tend to behave much better at war — one thinks of China, Vietnam, Latin America, when the exemplary behaviour of the Communist armies won over the population and thus won the war.)

Religion is an evil because it is actually, materially nothing more than an unprovable superstition which masquerades as a *good*, a cause, something worth fighting for, and far from bringing eternal life it brings early death and infinite rotting.

125

There has never been a war between those who believe in touching wood and those who believe in not walking under ladders; that's the kind of superstition you should give in to if the peasant in your soul can't do without moments of pure wallowing illogical mindlessness.

Yet beyond all the other religions, Catholicism annoys and appalls me; the oddness of, say, the Moonies is often pointed out by the media, and the weirdness of the Rastafarians, and the fanaticism of the Moslems — yet Catholicism is a sacred cow, despite the fact that its customs and conceits are easily as ludicrous. It is strange that this country has so little to say concerning the evils of Papism, considering how long and hard we struggled to break free of the straitjacket, and that the countries which threaten British territory are to a man Catholic — Catholic Ireland threatens Protestant Ireland, Argentina threatens the Falkland Islands, Spain threatens Gibraltar, Guatemala threatens Belize.

The arguments of certifiable Americans since the end of the Second World War have convinced the leaders of this country that the Soviet Union is its one and only enemy, but if they care to come down from their dream war of the worlds for a moment they may recognise that the USSR has never threatened one inch of British territory whereas Catholic countries threaten us every day — via hot air in the case of Spain and Guatemala, via slaughter in the case of Argentina. We have been wasting our time and ammunition facing up to the mythical Communist threat while a succession of Catholic nations have infringed upon our territories and, in the case of Northern Ireland, have made us look the most blundering, brutal, ineffectual country in Europe.

Yes, since the scare focus switched to Communism there has been little defending of the faith done. The Pope's visit last year was treated in an impossibly craven manner as every newspaper from the *Mirror* to the *Telegraph* queued up to kiss the Papal ring, and his constant facile pronouncements were drooled over by Fleet Street like the latest thoughts of Chairman Le Bon salivated upon by a posse of nine-year-old *My Guy* readers.

Whenever the Pope shows his wrinkled old pan he brings out

the forelock-tugger — not just in his own flock, whose natural habitat is in thrall — but in the Right-wing scribbling Establishment, the Bookers and Johnsons of the country who supposedly worship the Queen, the 'Defender of the Faith', above all; someone should remind the old boys that the 'Faith' referred to is Protestantism defended from Catholicism, *not* Capitalism defended from Communism. The Archbishop of Canterbury though, a regular guy who embodies all the Church of England's utter lack of hypocrisy and pomposity and is a war hero to boot, gets a consistently bad press when he is not being totally ignored; it seems that there is a masochistic, mystical streak a mile wide in this country, shown in the people by the second selling of Thatcher, shown in the Establishment by the adoration of the Pope, ancient enemy and modern supremo of everybody who just happens to want to trample on Britain.

Relatively respected writers such as Anthony Burgess write about him in excruciatingly homoerotic terms; words like 'virile' are thrown about because he drinks vodka until it's coming out of his ears (words like 'lush' would be thrown about if we were discussing an Anglican vicar, but with a Catholic from the Pope to the lowliest priest it is accepted as part of the whole hopeless, wallowing, pretty package) and used to be an actor (permanently 'resting'). And now, just like he was Jackie O, there will be a TV biography this autumn, three hours, five million smackers; he will be played by twice-divorced atheist Albert Finney, who in interviews calls him 'His Holiness' and drivels on about him as if he was Gerry Fitt or Che Guevara.

I have no doubt that it is only the pull of history and the credibility of tradition that prevents the Church of Rome from being held up to revulsion and ridicule in the way the Church of Moon is. There is, for instance, no Moonie practice so all-round weird and wacko as the habits of Opus Dei, an organisation to which the Pope last August gave the status of 'personal prelature', meaning that the head of Opus Dei in any of the 80 countries where it operates has the automatic rank of bishop and is no longer under the jurisdiction of the local Catholic hierarchy.

What this means in effect is that any maverick Catholic sicko is free to spread his poison wherever he wants without restraint from his regular church. Opus Dei was founded in 1928 by the Spanish priest José Maria Esvriva de Balaguer — the Spanish variety of Catholicism has always been particularly repellent, and when the Spanish people voted for a Republic in 1936 they were voting against the repulsive wealth and influence of the reactionary Spanish church, which backed Franco's Fascists to the hilt — whose theological masterpiece was THE WAY: 999 MAXIMS. My favourite is No. 208: *'Let us bless pain. Love pain. Sanctify pain. Glorify pain!'*

What people get up to in their own rooms is between them and their ironmonger, but this is complicated by the fact that Opus Dei runs a number of halls of residence, youth clubs and (get this) catering colleges in Britain, and nullified by the fact that Opus Dei recruits from the age of *14*. After a period of probation initiates are invited to lash themselves daily with a five-thonged whip, the 'discipline', and told of the purifying virtues of the cilis, a sort of miniature Iron Maiden which apparently does wonders for the soul if worn strapped to the thigh for a minimum of two hours each day.

It was amusing in the extreme to witness last year the *Daily Mail* campaign against the Church of Moon — 'The Church that breaks up families!' — fought out on front pages and in court rooms while on the editorial page there would be the latest in a long line of drivelling instalments concerning the healing power of the Catholic Church and its ability to thwart once and for all the monster mobsters in the Kremlin.

The family that flays together stays together, I suppose.

Guilt following unworthy actions is probably a good thing, but to tell a child that it was BORN BAD is the most wicked and worst start in life you can give anyone. It is an old joke about half the tarts in Soho being convent-educated, but it is a fact that the prison population of the UK holds a disproportionately high number of Catholics, and that a stunning number of drunks, dossers and other human flotsam were raised as Catholics.

Auberon Waugh got it right for once when he said: 'Traditionally, Catholics were taught that murder, prostitution

128

etc. were mortal sins. But so was missing Mass. Masturbation was as much a sin as rape, and you might as well be hanged for a sheep as a lamb. But in any case, if you made a good Confession, both were forgiven instantly.'

Catholicism is literally criminally irresponsible in the way it dictates that crimes against people (murder, rape) are no worse than being a naughty boy in the eyes of Big Daddy in the Sky; the Catholic is for ever a big baby, morally incontinent, messing himself, being cleaned up *ad infinitum*, powerless and proud of it — the IRA 'dirty protest' always struck me as quite dazzlingly typical Catholic indulgence with all the overtones of babyishness and self-loathing.

The basic Catholic gripe is that people are not anti-matter from the neck to the knees — as if the Big G did not know what he was doing when he drew up the plans! By being born biologically perfect you are Born Bad. Thus Catholic children are forced to Confession at an age when they have to invent sins because the sick old priest cannot believe that anyone is *good*. They make up fake sins, do fake penitence — chants easily as ludicrous as the much-ridiculed mantras of the Krishnamurti; again, a private punishment between you and Daddy G, no mention of making it up to the person, that other fellow unit of sin-ridden garbage you might have transgressed against. What a great birthright, what a standard to base life upon.

FOUR SONS FOUR KILLERS said the front page of the *Sun* awhile back, telling how a mother was dragged screaming from a courtroom after her fourth son had been jailed — 'What a family!' commented the judge — for a particularly vicious murder. 'Where did we go wrong?' sobbed the mother. 'We are strict Catholics.' It has been shown time and time again, from electric-shock-how-far-can-you-go psychiatry to concentration camp that if one group of people think another group of people have done something unspecifically 'bad' they feel very little compunction about destroying them — they feel justifed, sanctioned, they are even *proud of their work*; think of the meticulously-kept records of unspeakable atrocities the Allies stumbled across in Auschwitz. When you are brought up believing, as Catholics are, that people are born bad and remain

129

so, despite the massive evidence to the contrary — for every Nazi an Ally, for every vivisectionist a St Francis with a balaclava and a jemmy — then you will feel that the person you are killing had it coming all along, that you are an avenging angel. So simple, and so sick.

Everyone is born blank, and it is the easiest thing in the world to be good, or bad; if this biological truth was admitted by the Church of Rome, the churches would be empty, if everyone rejected mysticism and took complete responsibility for himself, the top-security gaols would be empty. 'The Devil made me do it!', the constant criminal's lament, is pure puny Catholic. The Catholic Church, by forgiving evil so easily — it has never come anywhere near excommunicating the butchers of the IRA, for instance — encourages evil behaviour. Only then can it be sure of full attendance, that it will be packed with guilty peasant morons shelling out their miserable pennies.

When murderers find God, it is the Catholic God — think of Hindley and Longford. Film stars and millionaires get Born Again. Auberon Waugh again: 'The modern Catholic Church often seems to be more of a social club for inadequates than a universal mission.' The leaders of the Church are of a horrifically low standard, from Pope Innocent of the Inquisition to today's 'Oh' Karol Wojtyla and his Chicago believers. His envoy Bruno Heim's recent extraordinarily violent outburst against Msgnr. Bruce Kent (one in a billion) and CND made perfect sense to me; nuclear weapons and Catholic doctrine are a match made in Hades — this world is corrupt, we are worthless, the only life worth living is the next one so let's get this two-bit dress rehearsal over QUICK. The plane that dropped the Bomb on Hiroshima was blessed by a priest. The kind of killing Catholics object to is abortion, more because they do not feel it is right for a woman to get away with sex — pushing a baby carriage is tantamount to wearing a dayglo sandwich board with the words I AM NOT A VIRGIN painted eight miles high — than out of a real concern with a denial of potential life.

Breed more, kill more; a grimly procreating dance of death. One thinks of the Maronite Christians of Lebanon — Fascist, Catholic and bloodthirsty; the bemedalled butchers of Latin

America; the IRA blowing the arms and legs off a seven-year-old sightseer at the Tower of London who was presumably part of the British imperialist war machine. Catholics are extraordinarily prone to Fascism: of the Catholic countries of Europe four of them — Spain, Italy, Portugal and Poland — have been Fascist this century, probably because they are both faiths based on bullying, pessimism and the suspension of all logic.

Catholicism is a disease that has historically affected the poor and ignorant and neglected, like tuberculosis, and thank goodness it is going the same way as the better part of the developing world shakes off religion — death's waiting room — and embraces the fight for life on earth ('Marxism — the only religion still making converts on a mass scale' — A.J.P.T., the History Superman). But it is also a slippery primeval chute down which the defeated, the suicidal but cowardly are prone to throw themselves; if it ever revives in Britain it will revive in Thatcher's Britain, because she brings out the defeated forelock-tugger in the once-proud worker.

The illogical quagmire of it finally attracts writers, because their brains tend to work overtime and it is a relief to take time off from thinking. Catholicism demands a regular and terrible suspension of the thought process — for instance, when the Communion bread is consumed, at the moment of mastication the food is actually thought to become the body of Christ ('Which makes the communicant a cannibal!' I quipped to my favourite lapsed Catholic — very witty, I thought). Like I say, all us wordsmiths need to take time out from brainstorm brilliance. I have my *Crossroads* — Greene, Waugh, Wilde, Spark have their cross, the only difference being that I laugh at my mindlessness and they are commandeered by theirs.

It is a million years since I digressed from the immediate subject to say the things that have needed saying for a long time concerning the Old Faith, the Old Folly, that need saying especially now when the assembled press of the Western World seems to tell me every day that the Pope should be king of the planet.

But only three years have passed since Mr Greene became a Catholic, and now it is 1929 and his first book *The Man Within* has been published. It met with 'inexplicable success'. Set in the eighteenth century, seething with Sussex smugglers, there are numerous killings, two suicides, one sex assault and general nastiness — start as you mean to go on: if it's mayhem it must be Graham. The epigraph — 'There's a man within me that's angry with me' is by Thomas Browne, and says it all: Francis Andrews is a *homo duplex*, and his tragedy, rather ordinaire and everyday as it seems, is the persona he wants to be compared with the person he is (what anyone other than a Papo-pessimist might call 'ambition'). Remember, this is not *really* Sussex but Greeneland; the hero cannot make an effort and *change*, but must wallow and whitter around waiting for a miracle — the miracle he finally gets is death, when he goes out in a blaze of glory by his own hand, ecstatic over having finally killed the nasty self.

Greene grew up on *Boys' Own* adventures, and this, his only historical novel, bears weak-kneed witness; it is obvious from Day One, or rather Book One, that Greene does not want to write rollicking good yarns but bloody dissections of the human soul. The smuggler is a smuggler in name only — *angst* does not translate well into a rural setting, nor into any century before this one (people were too busy to have *angst*) and 'Smuggler's *angst*' seems a particularly unlikely complaint — and in reality he is the prototype Greene hero, a post-First World War modern man who feels responsible for every cruelty that ever happened.

But there is a light at the end of the costume drama tunnel, and such a terrible light eyes never look upon. For the Thirties are here, and the stuff which Greene is made of — nightmares of crisis, failure and slaughter — is suddenly a passion play being acted out on the stage of the world. Men appear who could easily be Greene heroes; not the dictators who tower over the decade, but the weaklings, the collaborators, Chamberlain, Petain, Quisling. No single writer seemed so at home in the Thirties, not Steinbeck or Dos Passos or Warner or Hanley or Orwell, and the masterpieces bled out of him — *It's A Battlefield, England Made Me, Stamboul Train, The*

Confidential Agent, A Gun For Sale — as the wound he had cultivated since childhood chose this time to gape open.

In the Thirties the seeds of the most massive harvest of regret were sown, actions taken from which the most massive terror and guilt would surely result. It has often been said that the past is a foreign country, and to my mind certain decades *are* certain countries; the Forties were Russia, the Fifties were America, the Sixties were Britain, the Seventies were the united lands of the Arabs. The Thirties, God help them, were Greeneland.

'A kind of Russian roulette remained a factor of my later life, so that without previous experience of Africa I went on an absurd and reckless trek through Liberia; it was fear of boredom that took me to Tabasco during the religious persecution, to a leproserie in the Congo, to the Kikuyu reserve during the Mau-Mau insurrection, to the emergency in Malaya and to the French war in Vietnam. There, in those last three regions of clandestine war, the fear of ambush served me just as effectively as the revolver from the corner-cupboard in the life-long war against boredom.'

And so the Thirties, God help them, were Greeneland. In the fourth year of the decade of fear, Graham Greene's fifth book, *It's A Battlefield*, saw the dark light of day. *It's A Battlefield* is *the* terminal Thirties fairytale: ordinary people who have never met steered into hating and killing each other, individual happiness doomed by power, the bungled assassinations, England sleeping and waking up occasionally to deny that it has been having nightmares, Communism too young, not yet strong, just a tearaway in tears, a teenager in love.

The hero, Conrad, brother of a condemned man, a Communist who has killed a policeman, is aware constantly 'of the world humming and vibrating with the pulling of wires' — the condemned man's wife is every war bride — 'We were happy. It doesn't pay to be happy. I always told him it couldn't go on, but somehow we couldn't help it.' Shop of pawns, ship of fools — the wonderful Thirties, the good old days. Conrad is the Greene Man in full flower, fully developed from his

133

smuggling ancestors, a freak whose intelligence brings him nothing but the isolation, the solitary confinement of the soul that always goes with too much knowledge of the ever-loving, ever-rotting West: 'Brains, like a fierce heat, had turned the world to a desert around him, and across the sands in the occasional mirage he saw the stupid crowds, playing, laughing, and without thought enjoying the tenderness, the compassion, the companionship of love.'

If Greene's heroes are all one man, then his bit players are the most fascinatingly varied in fiction, and none more so than *It's A Battlefield*'s Mr Surrogate, the suave, sick Bloomsbury Communist. Despite his distaste for the hollowness of capitalism, Mr Greene did not follow the rest of the British literary exodus into what Stephen Spender called 'an arbitrary engagement with revolutionary left-wing politics' (usually expressed by fleeing to America on the outbreak of War between Britain and Germany — I guess you had to be there to understand it, heh heh), and wrote nastily of those 'for whom Intourist provides cheap tickets into a plausible future — my journey represented a distrust of any future based on what we are' (I think he means 'breathing'). Nevertheless he is fascinated by Communism, probably as an opponent (it is Communism not Catholicism which is now 'the only religion still making mass conversions' — little AJP! — after all) and understands it quite well.

The two faiths, Optimism represented by the Marxists and Pessimism represented by the Papists, are both based on a misanthropy, a loathing of life as it is; pessimistic misanthropy thinks the solution is death, and optimistic misanthropy thinks the solution is revolution. Communism in the Third World is usually a handy name for nationalism, pride, a desire to stop starving, a gut reaction, and is deliberately misunderstood by the West, but the phenomenon of white Western Communism is a genuine mystery to those who hate it. In the rich, bitter Mr Surrogate Mr Greene spells it out.

Communists, far from being naive and idealistic (the naive idealists have for a long time been the sole responsibility of the Right, and in my opinion the confused creatures of the British

134

National movements and parties and gangs are the most naive and idealistic beings ever to play at philosophers — such a superstition, that your skin colour is your destiny!), are brittle beings, almost bullet-proof; they spend their early lives seeing and feeling and suffering too much, suffering on behalf of everyone, until one day they wake up and the bruises are gone and the shell is there and they are perfect, Born Again, immune to depression and insanity and all those other ailments of the soft-centred aimless. The revisionist howl of all time is the Christmas cracker memo that says that Marshal Stalin was a Fascist dictator and not a Communist — not only was he a Communist, he was Supercommie, Everycommunist, the most colossal illustration of the Shell in action. One day Josef Stalin was a pock-marked, plodding, earnest and somewhat dull and sentimental young widower and the next day he was the Man of Steel, the man who would raise men who could bring Hitler to heel — without a doubt if one man has to be singled out of all those men of men who fought Fascism, Stalin was the man who saved the world.

Thus fastidious Mr Surrogate in his Bloomsbury rooms is a recluse who lives for revolution, a sadist who loves mankind, thrilled by his crusade to save the bus driver Jim Drover, a man whose touch would make him scrub his skin until it bled. 'In a cause was exhilaration, exaltation, a sense of freedom; individuals gave pain by their brutality, their malice, their lack of understanding.'

His seduction of Drover's young sister-in-law Kay — the promiscuous, glamorous, rebellious vessel into which Mr Greene pours all his appalled lust for the exotic, lurid, flytrap flower of young prole womanhood — is the coldest and the hottest ever committed to paper, and Kay herself, a male creation of the Thirties, *breathes*, you can smell the Parma Violets on her breath, and she makes the modern female creations of those numb American gnomes with the *names*, the Godforsaken names like Krantz and Jong, look just like the female-impersonating skeletons they are. Yes, this might be the best work of fiction you ever read in your life — but of course the worst always happens, as it always did in the Thirties.

It's A Battlefield is Greene's best, most realistic, least superstitious book, and it is possible that he scared himself with his commonsense, causing him to throw himself back into religion and other such illogical trash with a will. But his novels at their most lucid and disgusted do not point the way to change: YOU ARE HERE, they say like a bland department store map, SO SUFFER. I fear we must lay a good proportion of the blame for this apathetic attitude at the feet of Mrs Mary Goldberg, alleged virgin of Middle Eastern origin, later imaginatively remodelled by the Cathos as a whey-faced, simpering waif, but to a large extent the social philosophy of capitalism is all about keeping people lonely, isolated, thinking that their problems are unique to them rather than inherent in the buy and sell system (gorgeous Anna Raeburn's advice and ghastly Margaret Thatcher's enticements that you are NOTHING if you're not knocking yourself out buying the four flimsy walls you're contained in are sickening symptoms of the squeeze). Graham Greene bought the Big Lie — each man's struggle a separate one; as the Assistant Commissioner of *It's A Battlefield* says, 'Nobody cares about anything but his own troubles. Everybody's too busy fighting his own little battle to think of the next man.'

In a couple of years' time the best young men of Europe and America would leave everything they loved and go off to fight for the freedom of a faraway country of which they knew nothing but that it needed them. In the real world, though not in our world, men die for the freedom of other men every day of the week — but of course this spoils the depressive's peculiarly pure view of the world as one big sick jungle, it points to the extraordinary side of human nature: it is optimistic, and therefore corrupt.

While other men went to Spain to put things right, Graham Greene went to Liberia to find out what had gone wrong. The motive behind his Liberian trek was to get to the root of Evil, which he thought he would find in Africa in its raw state, untouched, pure — as though Africa, the raped continent, was still untouched in 1935! Liberia in particular cannot be treated as a primitive, instinctual society; it was founded in 1820 by the

American Colonisation Society as a country for freed slaves from the USA, and became a republic in 1847. The country is run by blacks of US origin and the language is the Queen's English. Lyme Regis is more primitive than Liberia.

In true depressive fashion Greene found the place hellish, but home: 'There seemed to be a seediness about the place you couldn't get to the same extent elsewhere, and seediness has a very deep appeal: even the seediness of civilisation, of the sky signs in Leicester Square, the tarts in Bond Street . . . It seemed to satisfy, temporarily, the sense of nostalgia for something lost; it seems to represent a stage further back.'

When not swooning with *nostalgie de la boue*, Greene was at death's door with a nasty case of tropical fever. What a sign from God this must have seemed to one as self-centred and superstitious as Greene! He was Born Again (again), discovering 'a passionate interest in living' where before he had assumed 'that death was desirable'.

In 1938 his Catholicism came to a pustulous purple head with *Brighton Rock*, a physically beautiful book made unattractive in that the male intellectual's attraction to the criminal is flaunted for the nth time. The intellectual, because of his circumstances and his circle of friends, is more unlikely than anyone to be a victim of crime — they're never murdered, they always kill themselves — leaving them free to craft beautiful but odious odes to criminals while the victim class, the working class, will aways defend to the death the death penalty. Hemingway and his bullshitting bullfighters, Mailer and Gilmore and Abbott, probably YOU and the Krays — one gets the impression that a massive majority of male intellectuals do in fact admire violent criminals very much, feel that they are in touch with their inner caveman selves in a way that a 'creative' (and therefore feminine — to create being female, to destroy male) man can never be.

To be a violent criminal — all action, no thought — seems to the intellectual, green(e) and naive as he is, to be a life of raw sensation and animal enjoyment. Of course violent criminals are the numbest, dumbest people on earth, but trying telling your sensitive young soul next door that, try tearing him away from his David Bailey pictures of the Kray twins long enough. Men have to make up their minds what they are, brains or brutes — they want it both ways. Personally I believe that too much thinking makes a man miserable, and I look forward to the day when every hunk is a lumberjack or something equally physical. Of course, I'm only joking . . .

Living outside of the law may be many things, Greene exclaims throughout *Brighton Rock*, but it is not BORING and therefore it cannot be really bad. A life of crime can get as monotonous as any other life when there is no other option, but of course well-connected Mr Greene wouldn't know that. He paints the hero Pinkie (Pinkie! A very likely diminutive for a murderous young thug. I suppose 'Basher' or 'Gnasher' would have introduced an unpleasant note of mindlessness into the tale) as more, not less than human; he has remained true to his horrid human nature, not cosied it up with the C of E and compassion, and therefore he is true to God.

Pinkie, poor brute, 17 and slum-bred and shot through with all the mind-warping poison of Catholicism, is obviously a suitable case for a social worker, a horrible end product of poverty and superstition and ambition, but Greene sees him as an animal, king of the Brighton jungle. Sean O'Casey called Pinkie Brown 'the most stupid and evil mortal a man's mind could imagine,' and it was the *stupid* that annoyed Greene — it is clear from the writing, the most sumptuous and sensuous ever committed to paper, that Graham Greene loves Pinkie Brown. 'The Boy', Greene calls him, as homosexuals will their youngsters. When he is not promoting Pinkie he is promoting the Catholic God, drooling on about him to such an extent that you want to shake him; it makes one sick to see this brilliant man reduced to the level of an old peasant crone squatting on the dirt floor of some adobe, mumbling almost unintelligibly to a non-existent creator — God looms over *Brighton Rock* like nothing so much as the rabbit in *Harvey*, a huge lie invented to stop someone's loneliness. At least there's a happy ending — Pinkie dies for somebody's sins, blinded by his own vitriol, the Bible according to St Dashiell.

In 1938 the Church snapped its fingers and Greene came running. The Church said 'Go' and Greene went, out to Mexico to report on the religious persecution there. It is a shame that his talents were not better employed putting his own Church in order by investigating the Catholic alliance with the Nazis in Spain, Italy and Poland and the increasingly heinous anti-Semitic sermons preached by the Roman Catholic clergy from pulpits in mainland Western Europe. Instead he went out and wasted his time and energy wagging a finger at brave, bullied little Mexico, and so the most stupid and shameful time of his life began.

Mexico has been trying to pull itself out of the mire since time immemorial — today it has still not succeeded, and it is not unusual upon the streets of Mexico City to see poverty-stricken men supporting their families by *setting their own mouths on fire*, for rich Americans to toss them coins. In the Thirties, showing the kind of courage and pride that is always known as Communism when it happens in Latin America, the Mexican government seized back American oil property and nationalised it.

This enforced programme of national pride took a strange turn in the remote southern areas of Tabasco and Chiapas where the local police force turned on the Church, closed down and destroyed churches and prohibited religious services. Of course Greene had to go and poke his nose in. His journey in Mexico resulted in his two dumbest books, *The Lawless Roads* and *The Power And The Glory*. Both are arguments for faith, the Catholic faith; but between the lines, in the invisible ink, both show the Catholic falling apart.

Here Greene is at Templo del Carmen, and he says: 'How could one grudge them the gaudy splendour of the giltwork, the incense, the distant immaculate figure upon the cloud? The candles were lit, and suddenly little electric lights sprayed out all around the Virgin's head. Even if it were all untrue and there were no God, surely life was happier with the supernatural promise than with the petty social fulfilment, the tiny pension and machine-made furniture.'

EVEN IF IT WERE ALL UNTRUE AND THERE WAS NO GOD! A

Catholic does *not* talk like this. Greene tries his hardest in these books to be a Catholic missionary, but he cannot even convert himself. Religion is advocated essentially as a cheap option to painkilling narcotics; capable of bringing solace to the hopeless, sleep to the restless. The morbidly sensitive side of him feels the pain of Latin America intensely; but the depressive, passive side of him holds no hope for a revolution, a change. Religion and opium have been mixed and matched in observation many times, but nothing illustrates the wicked deceptions that churches inflict on ignorant people more tragically than *The Lawless Road* — Mr Greene went to Mexico to praise Catholicism, but he buried it.

While Greene was sunning himself in Tabasco, something was breaking out in Europe that would prove the final grim antidote to his peculiarly passive, passionate depression — the War. War seems to be the only thing that can cure the depressive: he either shoots himself when war is declared or he cheers up. The suicide rate during any war takes a nosedive and the psychiatric wards empty overnight. Life is suddenly seen as a gift, not a prison sentence, and people pull themselves together, because they don't feel like piffling little individuals any more: they feel like a tiny part of something big, they feel like Communists.

War is a spectator sport for male intellectuals, so of course Mr Greene did not fight: instead he went into the Foreign Office, where he worked closely with Kim 'My Hero' Philby, who he loved and has never stopped loving (Greene writes in the wonderfully bold and brassy and unapologetic introduction to *My Silent War*). As it was for all who did not fight, the Second World War was a wonderful experience for Greene, who emerged from it at 41 finally a non-adolescent, no more a moaner, a man with perspectives. Like all British men of the time, he came out of the war years with an admiration for the Soviet Union that went as deep as his derision for the USA. As there are Communists who become deathbed Christians, so there are Christians who are obviously spottable as potential deathbed Communists. Mr Enoch Powell is one, and I think Mr Greene is another.

Those who survived the war were an evolved people, without superstition, without caste. In this country we saw this in the staggering landslide defeat of Churchill, whose image as saviour of his nation could not get over the fact that he was a Tory. In Greene the Black Dog finally seems to lift, and the all-pervasive pessimism becomes tempered with an echo of Anglican public school pigheadedness, a refusal to lie down and give up when Evil appears, a refusal to pray for redemption, but instead a stubborn will to look Evil curiously in the eye and go about cutting it down to size. Graham Greene did not gain a new faith in the Forties, but he lost an old one, which is a good start.

There was a final Papist blow-out in the appropriately-named *The End Of The Affair*, a banquet of betrayal, bitter lust and belief; then there were books about what capitalism, taken to its logical conclusion, does to people (*The Third Man, Dr Fischer Of Geneva*), and books about America, that terrible tumour on the planet, and what happens because America can only have enemies or banana republics — *The Comedians, Our Man In Havana, The Quiet American*. Now he lives in Cannes, where he conducts a savage and suicidal campaign against organised crime; never was a man in tax exile so noble.

There are several reasons why I wrote this, and why it's so long: to get YOU to read a book, birdbrain; secondly because Greene will soon be dead, by the will of some God or some gangster, and when he dies all the accolades will at last be poured on him, and he will probably replace the laughable Orwell as the recognised great British writer of the twent cent; to draw your attention to the fact that even if you never read Greene, a good deal of the great art of today — *Gorky Park, The Year Of Living Dangerously*, the songs of Elvis Costello — is set in Greeneland.

But mostly I suppose I wrote it because this country, for the first time, looks like Greeneland to me. The Commie-baiting clarion call to look out for 1984 was a lie all along; we've been living in Greeneland since the day we first elected Our Lady Of The Lash, and it is immeasurably worse. We do not live in a Soviet-style state which is always telling us to pull our socks up, strive onward, sacrifice ourselves for the greater good: we live in a country in which there are millions of tiny padded cells, and we are told that we must let life wash over us, let death come and live amongst us — we are as morally incontinent as we have ever been.

We have taken this moral incontinence from America — Reagan gibbering about a 'Holy War' against 'the focus of all evil' the USSR while his closest advisers whip callgirls and American nuns are murdered by American guns — who have shipped it out wholesale to us with their missiles, their herpes and their sick video films, all the other things America gives to countries better than it so it won't look like such a conspicuous pile of garbage any more. Through the curse of our common language we have taken the crap most cravenly, and we have lost ourselves. The people of this country have become superstitious peasants, sickeningly passive and unorganised, feeling the most tremendous powerlessness and unspecified pain and using the most extraordinarily destructive means to bludgeon themselves into unconsciousness.

This country calls itself Anglican, but it is not; it is merely adrift, and every so often it floats back into a Catholic mentality. This is not to say that the churches are filling up, or that young Catholics are not breaking away with as much verve and determination as ever, but it does mean that superstition, introspection and depression of a kind that is specifically Catholic has us in its grasp. From the cult of the self and the pain and ecstasy of aerobics and fasting to the self-inflicted mortifications of glue and sick video films, we are becoming mundane, morbid people, worthy citizens of Greeneland. As the people of that continent most butchered into submission by both America and religion, Latin America, read books, make weapons and stand up, we seem determined to take their place; the pride that we take in having a 'strong' leader, who mistreats us appallingly, is just one symptom.

Superstition is the root of all evil, and we are regressing constantly into the mists of brutish, violent superstition. The British think they can play with roles; leader, led, oppressor, freedom fighter, thinker, and always stop when they are bored. But these little games of domination and divine right have been going on too long, and are really eroding our capabilities to be anything *but* dominated. One day you'll wake up and you'll have forgotten how to say NO. One day we'll wake up and find out that the last exit from Greeneland is long gone.

Waiting for the Russian Ballet

When Mr Christopher Booker was in Moscow some years
ago, with the aim of making mincemeat of the Soviet
Union in general and the Russian Olympics in particular, he
chanced to travel on a bus, sitting behind two pretty, cheaply
dressed teenage bimbos who were discussing in English the
romantic attachment of a mutual friend. This is not unusual,
other people's love lives taking up at least 80 per cent of the
time, energy and thought processes of any normal decent
person — but what shocked and delighted the usually dour Mr
Booker about this discussion was the fact that these two cute
things were talking about their friend's dalliance in terms of
comparison with a similar situation in a novel by Mr
Dostoyevsky. This, he decided in a frenzy of reluctance, proved
irreparably that despite, *or because of*, the Russian people's
more *ordered*, shall we say, way of life, the working class of the
country were blessed with a refinement and appreciation of
your actual culture that the proletariat of the loose-living
Western countries could never have. When I was a pretty,
cheaply dressed teenage bimbo I could not *spell* Dostoyevsky,
let alone read him. But Soviet teenagers can and do, and their
parents queue for hours in the snow for tickets to the Bolshoi
with an enthusiasm that the working class of this country can
summon up only when queueing for the department store sales,
ready to go at Selfridges like a queue of pigs at a trough.

This cultural refinement of the proletariat, though most
striking in the USSR, can also be found in those countries
fortunate enough to have fallen under the benign influence of
the Bear, who are held tightly in his comforting iron grip. Let us
consider for a moment Eastern Europe, a most deliberately

misrepresented and misunderstood region. There was not much to be said in favour of Eastern Europe before it settled down with the Bear. People try and pretend that, before Communism, things were all hunky dory and democratic in the countries of the East, but this is just deceitful foolishness. Eastern Europe was a vicious, backward patchwork of fiefdoms, steeped in ignorance and quite hideous anti-semitism, sometimes literally Fascist (Pilsudski's Poland) to an extent that certain countries in the region (Hungary, Rumania) allied themselves with Nazi Germany during the war. Culture in Eastern Europe was practically non-existent before the countries got lucky enough to be kicked into shape by the Bear: pre-war Eastern Europe produced chi-chi Mr Chopin, the Gabor girls, Vlad the Impaler and Jayne Mansfield's second husband, hardly giants amongst men. Culture and art are neuroses, toxics which can only build up and be expelled properly in a fast and neurotic society, and these countries were simply too primitive for the process to go ahead. I do like the Africans, but it always makes me laugh to hear some Channel 4 talking head solemnly describe an African dancing around a huge phallic symbol as 'African Art'. African art! Come on! And your average Eastern European Joe did little more culturally than crouch by his dismal hearth scaring his friends with his vampire stories and perhaps occasionally, in a rare fit of jollity, fling himself about in the course of a colourful if monotonous traditional dance. ('Tradition' and *culture* are not the same thing, a common misapprehension.)

Of course this idyllic state of affairs could not continue after the most benevolent dictator the world had ever known, i.e. the Soviet Union, took an interest in its surly peasant neighbours and set its mind on civilising them. Even the Poles, the most profoundly unintelligent, ungrateful and sullen people on earth, were given State film schools at which to polish their grudges. What a mistake that turned out to be! Spectacularly untalented as a race — did you see *The Jeweller's Shop*? And *he's* their most infallible — given to equal parts sadism and sentimentality like all Papists, they set to work with a will making their horrible films about sulking and psychopaths, not one song and dance routine or happy ending between them. All the dissident artists of Eastern Europe, from Kundera to the Plastic people, make exactly the sort of whingeing, existential, idiot art that the short back and brains of the new Right, who whine so long and hard about these people's freedom to express themselves as they please, would complain about incessantly as symbolic of twent cent wet liberal decay if it had been produced by indigenous British artists. The archetype Eastern bloc émigré rebel artist is that Bohunk who last year *wrapped a formation of Florida islands in Schiaparelli pink polythene* to the tune of three million dollars. And this, believe it or not, was his masterpiece.

'If we had shot a few writers,' commented cute Mr Khrushchev during the Hungarian temper tantrum, 'this would never have happened.' It is this regrettable attitude on the behalf of the Communist leaders, that these pathetic, would-be intellectuals really are dangerous to the Communist monolith, that has caused the excitable knee-jerk Soviet-baiters of the West to seize upon a few grossly under-talented hacks in an effort to play cerebral soldiers, to feel as though they are actually squaring up against the might of the Red Army. This state of affairs is less objectionable than pitiable, and was most keenly and poignantly visible in the Western intellectual's old-fashioned rough trade crush on La Walesa — who was actually a major eastern bloc cultural artefact in that he gave the impression of having listened to far too many smuggled Bruce Springsteen records before going right out and creating himself as his own masterpiece, a monument to be proud of, throbbing, untamed peasant manhood, and about as relevant to contemporary realpolitik as a Flat Earther.

The Russians have actually done the professional whiners of Eastern Europe a very good turn by harassing them, in that if they were not products of satellites of the big bad Bear no one would ever have heard of them, they are so uniformly unremarkable. Persecution is their publicist, bleating for attention their vocation. And now, due to the unbearably sloppy and ill-sorted thought patterns of the west *vis-à-vis* the USSR, the word 'dissident' has become interchangeable with the word 'genius'.

The whole subject of the alleged cultural domination of

Eastern Europe by the Soviet Union is so tiny-minded and petty in terms of real world agony and conflict that only one aspect of it is directly offensive as opposed to pathetic. And that is the enthusiasm of woolly-minded and feeble Western thinkers to weep and drool over the plight of artists in the Bear's backyard while apparently not giving a damn about the appalling lives led by the people of Central America, which due to the fears and paranoias of the USA is little more than one big abattoir. I would love to know why the lively, physically attractive people of El Salvador have less right to live than the sluggish, ugly Polacks; I would love to know why the artists of Eastern Europe deserve the freedom to shoot their mouths off endlessly, while the people of Central America do not deserve the freedom to protest about their right to eat three meals a day without being called Communists and shot on the spot. The first and final freedom is the freedom to eat, not to create, and this is a freedom that those people under Russia's protection — unlike those under America's — have never been without since the end of the war.

So onward, onward, ever Westward — it cannot be too long now until even this ridiculous, chintzy excuse for a sovereign state gets lucky enough to fall under the hell, sorry, HEEL, of the glorious, gory, gallant Russian jackboot. And what wondrous mutations will our tacky, toothless old culture go through then! Goodbye to all those rotten boring statues of dead, useless Sloanes that litter London like drab showroom dummies two centuries out of date; hello to the heroic representations of the honest working man's remarkable routing of the Nazi beast during the last war. Goodbye to the ridiculous, American-inspired sight of young negroes breaking their necks while attempting to spin on their heads, aloha to the all-night queues for the ballet. Best of all, goodbye to the alcoholic, lower-middle-class, morally incontinent Tory yokels who pass for writers and journalists at the moment, and hello to nice, neat, well-behaved little Party hacks, who do not pretend for a minute to be independent thinkers and who get on with the business of singing the praises of their paymaster while living in one of those dinky writers' blocks (in Russia a writers' block is

147

somewhere where one lives, rather than something one pretends to have in order to get out of working) and summering in one of those bijou coastal dachas awarded by the state to those particularly subservient scribblers.

There is nothing wrong with any country on earth that is so serious that it cannot be cured by a ruthless Russian invasion followed by a brutal suppression of all dissent. There are many reasons why I shall be out on the street garlanding the brave boychiks of the Red Army when they finally get here, and the desire to survey a proletariat culturally refined to the degree that they can look at a man in ballet tights without giving in to the irresistible urge to titter and point at the merchandise is one of them.